TODAY'S INSPIRED LATINA™

Volume VIII

LIFE STORIES OF SUCCESS IN THE FACE OF ADVERSITY

JACQUELINE S. RUÍZ

Today's Inspired Latina

For more information, contact:

Fig Factor Media, LLC | www.figfactormedia.com
Today's Inspired Latina | www.todayslatina.com

Cover Design & Layout by Juan Pablo Ruiz
Printed in the United States of America

ISBN: 978-1-952779-48-0

Library of Congress Number: 2020947454

I dedicate this volume to all the authors who have previously participated in *Today's Inspired Latina*, as well as the sponsoring corporations and individuals who have shown their undying support for this amazingly inspiring mission.

Table of Contents:

Acknowledgements

As always, my heart is filled with gratitude for the people surrounding me who bring my dreams to fruition.

First, I want to thank my production team. Thank you to Gaby Hernández Franch, who managed all areas of the project so smoothly, and Karen Dix, the official editor of the *Today's Inspired Latina* series, who has been with me since Volume I. And to Juan Pablo, the love of my live and graphic designer—I can always count on you to elevate the beauty of every project you touch.

Finally, I would like to thank all the participating authors who believed in the series and courageously chose to share their stories. I know their words will continue to inspire and elevate for generations to come.

- JACQUELINE S. RUÍZ

Introduction

This year has been one for the history books. However, in times of crisis, I'm able to take stock in all I have already survived—two bouts of cancer, childhood tragedy, business challenge, harrowing landings as a pilot—and pool my emotional resources to move forward. The pandemic was no exception. And for me, moving forward with *Today's Inspired Latina Vol. VIII* has been a ray of sunshine in an otherwise bleak year.

Thank goodness for these wonderful stories of inspiration and hope, that are perhaps needed more now than ever before. Even as our country battles the pandemic and weathers a turbulent economic and political climate, the insight of these authors is drawn from their reservoirs of positivity and hope. Listen closely to their messages and you will see that they give us a virtual roadmap to become our best and weather any storm, including COVID-19.

This volume returns us to authors from the U.S. and Canada after featuring European authors in *Today's Inspired Latina Vol. VI* and Latin American authors in *Today's Inspired Latina Vol. VII*. The authors within these pages, like those who have preceded them in other volumes, bring their own magic to the project. They fill these pages with their energy, light, and love, and it never ceases to amaze me how their stories reach off the page to touch the hearts of those who read them.

Yet, I see something unique in the authors within Vol. VIII. Each one is bringing their unexpected magic and beautiful energy to service a group or community, and it's wonderful to behold. It fills my heart with an indescribable feeling of gratitude to know they are each serving the world in their own personal way. It makes me all the more grateful they came forth to share their stories, and I am able to help deliver them to the world.

As always, I am humbled and honored to present this volume of *Today's Inspired Latina.* Enjoy!

Preface

BY PATRICIA MOTA

I was in high school when I first noticed the inherent inequities that exist in this country for educational access, resources, and opportunity. Before my junior year, I went from attending school within my predominantly Mexican/African American and low-income neighborhood on the Chicago/ Indiana border, to a predominantly Caucasian and more affluent community outside of Phoenix.

What a difference. Instead of military recruiters, the school was regularly visited by several college recruiters. I met regularly with guidance counselors to make college plans and enroll in courses with advanced academic rigor, like AP physics and calculus. And, I recognized that my access and opportunity to these advantages was strictly based on the socioeconomic status of the community. It was an eye-opening experience, and one where I realized my personal passion towards becoming an advocate for access and equity.

My personal experience is shared by many Latinas today, including many of the contributing authors in the *Today's Inspired Latina* series. Unfortunately, denial of access to opportunities doesn't stop when we graduate high school or even when we begin our professional career. I, like many from underrepresented groups, have had the experience of being passed over for a promotion or not allowed an opportunity simply because of the institutional structures and biases that hinder progression for people like me.

My role at HACE (Hispanic Alliance for Career Enhancement) has helped me work toward healing these inequities. I'm dedicated to opening up doors to access and opportunity. One group that we serve is Latinas and women via the National *Mujeres de HACE* Women's Leadership Program. I know that Latinas are fearless when it comes to reaching their highest potential if they are given the opportunity and the proper support to unleash their talents. They know how to never lose sight of their goal, and they generously embrace their responsibility to pay it forward on the job and within their communities.

I'm happy to report this courage and determination is manifesting in a gradual, but persistent, shift of Latinas entering more professional workspaces and into leadership ranks. Also, more Latino students are completing high school and college than ever before, and college enrollment increased from 35% to 47% between 1996 and 2016.

For many young women among the demographic, they will graduate from college and may even serve as the first in their field, becoming an important role model for the next generation. The power of seeing someone who looks like you succeed in your chosen profession cannot be underestimated. That's why HACE is committed to helping Latinos succeed in every phase of their careers and to know that achieving an entry level position is the starting point, not the goal.

However, we won't get anywhere if we don't see changes in the workplace. Today, more and more companies and leaders are waking up to the reality that a diverse, equitable, and inclusive workforce leads to new ways of thinking, more informed decision-making, and better business results. Latinas typically bring the much-needed values of humility, family first, and adaptation into the mix. We remind the corporate world that we can all move up the ladder and attract top talent together, as long as we are both sensitive to the needs of the other.

I know as Latinas we experience pressure to blend in and hide what makes us unique, but I tell those entering the corporate world that it's critical to bring your authentic self to work every day, and learn when to adapt, not assimilate, and to be effective. The most successful people are those who feel comfortable in their skin and can focus exclusively on their own development and success.

The problem is reversible. A recent study by the Center for Talent Innovation showed that 76 percent of Latinos repress parts of their persona at work due to the fact that they do not feel they can bring their whole selves to work, or because they don't see themselves reflected in the leadership at their organization. Just imagine how empowering it would be if they did!

As an effort to move the needle, HACE provides leadership programs which cater to empowering Latinx, and unleashing their potential and overall authentic leadership. Specifically, we offer the *Mujeres de HACE* women's leadership program, which is now in its 12th year.

The program has empowered nearly 1,500 women nationally to grow professionally, break down barriers, and succeed, where 70 percent obtain a promotion and increase in pay less than 12 months after completing the program. We are proud to have national sponsorship from Allstate, AT&T, American Express, JLL, Marathon Oil, Nielsen, NBCUniversal, PayPal, and others who are dedicated to making a real impact on women's careers.

From this leadership framework, I found Jackie Camacho-Ruiz, who shares the same burning desire as myself, to empower Latinas and offer them access to greater opportunity. By providing a platform to tell their stories in *Today's Inspired Latina*, these brave women share their experiences of taking that leap of faith to achieve the next level of personal or professional success—whatever it may be for them. It's incredible to see so many *Mujeres de HACE* alumnae featured on *Today's Inspired Latina* platform!

I believe you should never underestimate the power you have as one person. So many times, we think it will take armies and troops, someone with a lofty title or in a high position, to make a difference. In reality, it starts with YOU as a caring individual who is unafraid to take action to move toward a personal mission.

It takes EACH of US to truly realize the full potential of ALL of us! United we are stronger and can better meet our potential, as long as we support each other in the journey. HACE is one way we do it. *Today's Inspired Latina* is another. Be unafraid, unapologetic, and unleash your potential by taking action today!

Patricia Mota
President & CEO
Hispanic Alliance for Career
Enhancement (HACE)

Araceli Zanabria

"We are what we decide to achieve."

Some people are born with the opportunity to achieve their goals without much difficulty. Others have to make bigger efforts and dedication to achieve their success. At the end of our existence, we are what we decide to achieve.

BENNY

Every day at 5:30 a.m., my internal biological alarm woke me up and I had just two hours to get Benny ready for his therapy. Ever since he was born, and for 18 years thereafter, I committed myself to giving him the quality of life that he deserved. Every day of his existence, I was honored to facilitate his daily rituals, from brushing his teeth to tying his laces. By 7:30 a.m., the bus picked him up and he had to be ready! He knew he was leaving but he also knew I was there for him if he needed me. His customized wheelchair weighed 120 pounds and Benny weighed 50 pounds, but I could lift more if it was necessary to get him where he needed to go!

Benny Jr. was a handsome boy, afflicted with cerebral palsy, but filled with life and happiness. He went to a special school throughout his 18 years, where he received the therapies and activities necessary for him to have an active social life in accordance with his disability. I consider myself very fortunate to be surrounded by good people with big hearts who cared for my child during his classes, and who participated alongside my family at his christening, first communion, graduations, and birthdays.

During the time Benny was at school, I did my daily activities. My English class started by 9 a.m. and finished at noon. After class, I delivered perfume orders to the hospitals and to Clinique, where I knew many of Benny's caregivers, and those who referred me to them. Around 2:30 p.m., I hurried back to prepare a meal for Benny, and I fed him. Most of us have a meal in about 20 minutes, but my son Benny leisurely enjoyed his over the course of an hour.

The afternoons were very happy for Benny, surrounded by love and care, including the happy moments beside his brother Irving. Benny loved music and I always knew what type of music he was in the mood to hear. My family and friends always asked me how I knew what he liked or disliked, but I assumed that was the result of a great bond between mother and son.

At night I brushed his teeth, and after taking his medicines, Benny went to sleep.

Benny slept in my bedroom the last eight years of his life. Often, he would wake up at night or just not sleep at all. I looked after him and changed his position to avoid sores being formed on his body, or I would talk to him to calm him down. Regardless of whether I was tired or slept only for a few hours, I got up and got ready for work.

When Benny was a baby, his father Benito had an evening job, so we had the flexibility to work and take care of our children without a babysitter. After a few years, Benny and Irving's father got another job working during business hours, so I had to adjust my work schedule to meet Benny's medical appointments and Irving's school activities.

Until the age of 10, we could not leave my son Benny in the care of a babysitter, due to his condition and special needs. Fortunately, I was able to hire a very reliable and wonderful person to babysit my children after school. Chanita took care of my sons for eight years.

I have described a typical day in my life with my son Benny, but it was my life and I was able to do it. Can you do your life when the going gets tough? And will you?

At the age of 18, my son Benny died as a result of his medical condition. To date, it is painful not to have him with me, but it comforts me that he is resting from the physical condition that kept him confined to a wheelchair.

IRVING

Throughout our lives, we encounter difficulties that cause us pain and sadness. This was the case of my second son, Irving, when he was 17 years old. He went to the doctor for an annual physical checkup and his doctor told us that he had a hernia which needed to be removed. During the preparation for the surgery, the surgeon found another medical problem.

He sent Irving to receive specific tests to rule out the

presence of cancer. Unfortunately, the tests were positive. On November 5, 2011, my son Irving was diagnosed with cancer, and we were consumed with stress and uncertainty because we didn't know whether the cancer had spread to other parts of his body.

It was a great relief when the doctor notified me that the cancer was contained. I was so proud of Irving's positive attitude and strength throughout the whole diagnosis, the surgery to remove the cancer cells, and, most of all, throughout his chemotherapy treatment. He gave me the strength not to fall into those moments where I felt devastated, thinking that I could lose my second child.

When Irving got sick, he was only six months away from graduating from high school. He was very brave, despite being weak and in pain. He attended school, and sometimes I had to pick him up two hours after he arrived. His teachers and classmates were very supportive during his four months of chemotherapy. Irving's high school doesn't allow students to wear hats, however they made an exception with Irving because he completely lost all his hair during the chemotherapy treatment. His teachers, staff, and classmates dedicated one day in his honor called "Hat Day." All of his classmates and teachers wore a hat to show their support for Irving. I will always be grateful to everyone for making my son feel so special!

I remember the day when my son finished his chemotherapy treatment and said something that I will never forget. *What doesn't kill you makes you stronger.* By the time Irving graduated from high school, his health had improved greatly, and new hair grew back.

To date, my son Irving is cancer free. He is 25 years old and graduated from college with a degree in public relations.

ARACELI

I was born and raised in Michoacán, Mexico. I graduated from the University of San Nicholas of Hidalgo with a bachelor's degree in agricultural engineering and came to this great country full of dreams in the late 80's as an immigrant. Because English was not my primary language, acclimating was a struggle, but learning the language was just the beginning of a countless list of small, but realistic goals to improve my life and, eventually, the lives of my children as well.

Namely, I had to fulfill my role as mother and caregiver for Benny with his special needs, and also help Irving develop his abilities and live a normal life. However, I also had my own goals. I started studying ESL in 1995 while taking a computer course. I also had a perfume sales business, and my customers were people I spoke with every day about Benny's medical condition, like nurses, secretaries, therapists, and people who were referred by my clients.

Over the years I have had ups and downs, but never had the intention to stop achieving new goals. On the contrary, I strongly believe that we learn from both good and bad experiences. The biggest reason to improve myself was to offer a better life to my children. I woke up every day with the conviction to fulfill all activities on my list.

When Benny was three months old, I promised him that he

would see and enjoy life through me. That was my promise to my son, and I fulfilled it until his last breath. The love for my children made me develop a skill and great strength to stay positive and alert. I firmly believe that love is the greatest emotion we have, and it can help us achieve even the most unimaginable in life.

My perfume business lasted for eight years until I decided it was time to move on to my next goal: to obtain my real estate license. At that time, I did not understand much English; however, I would not let it be an obstacle to pursue my dream of becoming a real estate agent. It was difficult, but I set out to achieve it. I went to school at night while I received training in a real estate office. Of course, it was very stressful to combine caring for my children with special needs, spending time in the office, and attending school at night. Although some people did not believe I could do it, I always had the conviction to reach my goals. I can proudly say that I passed the exam to receive my real estate license on the first attempt. Then, exactly one year later, I passed my exam to become a licensed real estate broker.

After three years working as a real estate agent with my mentor, I decided to open my own real estate office. To date, I have been working as a realtor for 18 years, specializing in residential sales in the Bronx and lower Westchester County in New York.

Good service always leaves a mark on customers and the desire to refer me to their family and friends. I really enjoy my job, and the best part in the process of buying and selling properties is seeing the smile on the face of my clients when they receive the keys of their new home. I can proudly say that to date, I enjoy the friendship of many of my former clients.

I've been living in New York City for more than three decades, and through the years I've owned different types of businesses to create employment opportunities in the area. Aside from being an agent, I am also a real estate investor.

Despite the bad experiences I endured as my sons struggled with their physical conditions, there were many moments full of joy, birthdays, and happy celebrations. So, too, my own life and experiences in the U.S. have brought me happiness, and I continue to grow in my career, alongside the love and support of my family. I truly believe that our dreams can come true if we pursue them with consistency and persistence. I was able to achieve many of my goals and so can you!

REFLECTION QUESTIONS

1. What goals do you keep working towards, even when the going gets tough?

2. What helps you stay focused and working towards your goals, even when time is short, or "life" interferes?

3. Who are you consistently "there" for, no matter what they require you to do?

BIOGRAPHY

Araceli Zanabria has been a real estate agent and investor in the State of New York for the past 18 years and specializes in residential sales throughout the Bronx and lower Westchester County. She is an active member of the National Association of Hispanic Real Estate Professionals (NAHREP) and serves as treasurer of the Bronx chapter board.

In her spare time, Araceli enjoys spending quality time with her family, and giving back to society as a volunteer for Make A Wish Foundation (MAW), where she works with families whose children are chronically ill. She facilitates the communication between families and the staff of MAW Foundation. She loves seeing the big smiles on each child when their wish comes true!

Araceli Zanabria
aracelirealtorteam@gmail.com
(917) 518-5728

Evelyn Rodriguez

"Let go without looking back."

Success and accomplishment can only be achieved with determination. Those two words, success and accomplishment, were my driving force as I grew up.

As a little girl, I dreamed of one day becoming some kind of professional. I watched my mother working hard and struggling for years in factory jobs. I was very proud of her, but it was so painful to see her work so many grueling hours.

A ROCKY START

I was raised in an environment with all types of abuse. Before my parents met, they both had moved from Puerto Rico to Chicago to chase the American Dream. My mother met my father at the post office at the age of 17. They got married a year later. Another year later, I came into the picture. Three years later, they had my sister. My earliest childhood memories of my parents were mostly of my mother crying every weekend because my father would leave on Friday and not come back until Monday. I remember them arguing and talking about "another woman" all the time.

My last memory of my parents was when I was five years

old. My mother finally left my father and got divorced on the grounds of emotional, physical abuse, and adultery. My mother worked very hard to give my sister and me everything we needed, making sacrifices for us at her expense.

Later, my mother remarried and lived with her partner for 18 years. Although he was a great provider, he was regularly unfaithful to my mother. My mother worked nights, and he would take care of us. Her second husband was supposed to be a father figure to us, but instead he sexually abused my sister when she five years old and me when I was eight years old. We never told my mother because we were scared to lose her. My mother finally left him and decided to move us to Puerto Rico.

My sister and I did not know about each other's experiences with my stepfather until we were teenagers. She was having nightmares every night about being abused. For so long, I blamed myself for not protecting my little sister, but I had no idea what was going on and could not even understand that I was also a child.

I was 16 years old when we moved. That year was a year of so many changes. We started new schools, and we did not even know how to write in Spanish. It was such a huge difference in culture from Chicago to Puerto Rico. It took us a while to adjust to our new lives on the island, but we did have peace. My mother was a single mother, and we never received financial assistance from our dad.

PAINFUL CHANGES

I graduated from high school and met the man who I

thought I would love forever. We dated for a year and then we got married. I was 18 years old and a freshman in college at the time, but he did not approve of me going to school, so I dropped out. I could not have friends. I could not talk to anyone on the phone. He did not want my family to come over because I told them he was mistreating me.

My mother decided to tell him to change his ways, and he banned her from visiting us. I struggled with my weight constantly, and he would mentally and physically abuse me all the time. I eventually wanted to have a family, so we decided to move to Chicago to find help. After visiting a fertility center for nine years, I finally got pregnant.

Even though I was in an abusive relationship for 10 years, I thought bringing a child into our marriage would make things better. I don't know what I was thinking. I wanted to leave him, but I was too scared to do it. On a daily basis, he would threaten to kill me if I ever left him, and I truly believed him.

I never wanted to share the problems we had, and the abuse I faced, with my family because of everyone's prior experience. I kept quiet about my marriage for a long time. I did not break the cycle; all I knew was how to be a product of my environment.

My life changed when my daughter was six months old and we were in the car with her father. He was drunk and swearing, and I asked him to take us home. As we were driving, I kept saying to myself, "There is no way I will allow my child to live and grow up in this environment." I prayed and prayed and asked God to help me get out. That experience, along with God's grace, gave me the strength to no longer be afraid and let go without looking back. That is exactly what I did.

I filed and paid for a divorce and left the house. He returned to Puerto Rico and we never heard from him again. He never helped us financially; he was completely out of our lives. I was determined to succeed on my own and give my child a better life.

I was so adamant about school, my career, and giving my daughter a good life that I sacrificed quality time with her in return, even though I knew that leaving him was the best thing I could do. I remember driving her to her sitter every morning, crying as I listened to the song by Will Smith, *Just the Two of Us*. I listened to this song for months. It was my daily reminder that all I was doing was for her. I know I loved her more than life itself. She meant the world to me.

CHANGES FOR THE BETTER

I was working at Bank of America as a teller at the time, and I enrolled in Triton College. At work, I was trying to get certified in all banking roles and was promoted nearly every year. I was so dedicated and such a hard worker! In 2005, I finished my associate's degree, taking only part-time classes for six years.

I decided I was not going to stop. I enrolled at Dominican University where I finished my B.S. in organizational leadership 2007. I was given a grant from Barat's Scholarship for having good grades. One of the proudest moments in my life was walking down the stage to get my master's degree in 2009. It was also one of the saddest moments, realizing I would not come back to the place that gave me so much knowledge. It was totally rewarding to be an adult learner because I was ready to be a top achiever. I had a 4.0 GPA and I was a Phi Theta Kappa.

Education has been important to me because I was a first-generation college graduate and the only one in my family with a master's degree. I was so proud of myself because I was able to achieve this with so many struggles and challenges. I decided to celebrate my accomplishment by throwing a big party for myself. I even had signs made for the lawn. I always told myself that education is the only thing no one can take away from you. I broke the cycle.

After having so many difficulties, even getting an apartment as a single mom, I was saving to buy a house. I did not qualify by myself, even though I had a good down payment. I had to add my sister on the mortgage application in order to purchase my first home, which was an apartment building with two flats, located in Chicago. I was still able to send my daughter to private schools through her high school graduation.

I decided to work on my other obstacle, which was my weight. For years, I went on every diet I heard about. The weight struggle was real. I would go up and down constantly, from losing ten pounds to gaining twenty. I went to the health club a few days a week.

I decided to have a gastric bypass after reaching 292 pounds. This was so painful and caused many challenges. Even today, I still have health issues. Being overweight is such an emotional struggle. You feel ugly, misunderstood, and unaccepted. You hide from the world. You have no confidence. You're always hiding your depression about your weight.

Eventually, I lost more than 100 pounds which changed my life. For the first time, I felt good about myself. I sold my apartment building and bought a home close to the city with a big pool and a playhouse.

In 2011, I signed up at Triton College to get certified as a Spanish interpreter in the legal, education, and medical fields and I completed the program in 2013. I then started interpreting on my days off for the Health Justice Project at Loyola, assisting patients with their medical conditions, and letting them know about the programs offered to help low income individuals in the community. I also get called occasionally by Access on Time language services to interpret for patients.

Meanwhile, my career continued to bloom at Bank of America. I became a branch manager and assistant vice president. Even though the company paid for my education, and I was thankful, I needed a change. Bank of America had made so many changes to its sales structure, I felt like a car salesman, and this was definitely not my calling. I decided to look elsewhere, and I interviewed for a community bank and was hired.

A year later, Wintrust acquired us. Wintrust has given me the best experience I have ever had in banking. They have taught us to be very involved in the community and to give back. I have built great relationships and am proud to work for a company that has the same beliefs I do.

I remarried and had a beautiful daughter, but I have a very

low tolerance for relationships after my past one and things did not work out. We parted after 10 years together. I am grateful that he is a good father, and we have a good relationship because of our daughter. She currently attends St. Petronille School in Glen Ellyn, near my work.

My oldest daughter is married to a Marine and is studying to get her degree while working as a Veterinarian Technician. She just made the Dean's list. I also have two grandbaby puppies. The family is living on a base in North Carolina, and I am extremely proud of them!

A GLANCE AT LIFE

I have no regrets on this journey that I have lived. It has made me a stronger, confident woman. It has made me a better person who is grateful for everything I've learned. It also reminds me that God has been great to me.

I strive daily to make sure I truly make a difference with everyone I touch. My last goal would be to someday complete my PhD in organizational leadership.

I will leave you with this acronym, YTTF dear to my heart:

Y – Yesterday, I was a young girl with many struggles and far away dreams.

T – Today, I am a successful woman who has been able to accomplish many of her dreams.

T – Tomorrow, I will continue to give to others and make a difference with the lives I touch.

F – Forever, I will never forget where I came from and hope to be an inspiring Latina to others.

I end here with the wise words of Frida Kahlo which I have found to be true in my own life: "At the end of the day, we can endure much more than we think we can."

REFLECTION QUESTIONS

1. What journey in your life has made you stronger?

2. What is the most important goal that you want to achieve?

3. What is your driving force?

BIOGRAPHY

Evelyn Rodriguez was born in Chicago and is the branch manager, vice president of Glen Ellyn Bank & Trust and Wintrust Community Bank. She has been in banking for more than 31 years. She is passionate about helping others reach their goals. She has two girls, ages 12 and 24.

She received her associate's degree in applied science in human resources management and earned her B.S. in business administration. She completed her M.S. in organizational leadership with a concentration in the Women's Leadership Program. She was a Barat Scholar for Dominican University and featured in Todays Chicago Woman magazine.

In 2011, she was certified as a Spanish interpreter in the legal, medical, and education fields. She has been a Spanish interpreter for the Health Justice Project at Loyola, assisting low- income patients with their medical conditions. In her free time, she currently interprets for patients at Access Language Services.

Evelyn was a professional advisor for DePaul University and a mentor for Chicago Public Schools. She is currently a board member of the Glen Ellyn Chamber of Commerce.

Evelyn Rodriguez
evy1221@gmail.com
773-551-364

MariCarmen Ortiz-Conway

"When you chase your dreams, magic happens."

Sometimes, to relieve homesickness, all you need is a little piece of home. I left Mexico as a young bride to move to the United States with my husband. While I was sad to leave my family, I was excited to start my new adventure. I took with me my strong faith and prayed that God, as well as his Blessed Mother, Our Lady of Guadalupe, would guide me to wonderful things.

FITTING IN

We settled in St. Louis in 1992, as newlyweds. My husband and I built our family over the course of eleven years and had four beautiful boys. I loved being pregnant and having children. I took good care of myself by eating well and exercising plenty. My children know their Mexican heritage and speak Spanish as well as English. They are the loves of my life and made my transition to this country so much easier, but for years I still felt a strong pull to return to Mexico. I missed everything about it—the cuisine, the culture, the colors, and the abundant, warm sunshine. I especially missed my family and friends.

I had no past in my new country, which made it difficult for me to connect with other parents. At sporting events, people were polite, but I felt we had very little in common. In Mexico, when I met someone, I usually was able to foster an instant connection over something, whether it be a person, place, or experience.

In St. Louis, things felt awkward. Despite this, there was always one place I could take myself back to in Mexico—the kitchen. Cooking connected me to my past with wonderful, sensual, memories, like the fragrant smells wafting from my aunt's oven during the holidays, and the mouthwatering taste of my grandmother's "green" fettuccini. Food was a piece of happiness for me, and my recipes awakened my senses while helping me revisit beloved days gone by. I shared this happiness with my new friends, and I loved the looks on their faces when they tried a new flavor or recipe. This was how I began connecting with others, and in return, they opened the doors to their hearts and homes.

Cooking is an art form that has unexpectedly taught me many lessons. For instance, I have learned that most everything can be fixed. When I add too much salt to a recipe, I creatively add ingredients until it is even better than I originally planned. In this way, the kitchen can mirror life. Through our love and passion, hope and creativity, we can fix our mistakes and move on, sometimes ending up better than we had originally planned.

I began providing teacher luncheons for Catholic Education week at my children's schools. Then, one day, I brought some tamales to the secretaries at school as a 'thank you' for their hard work. They loved them so much that they asked me to make more for the CFO of the school whose wife was sick and going through a difficult time. I did so, and shortly after that, a friend asked me to cater a local food fest called Creve Coeur Days, an event attended by 5,000 people. I was amazed and nervous to accept, but my friends were persistent. Without knowing how I was going to do it, I said yes, but quickly panicked. Where was I going to prepare food for that many?

When the CFO found out I was catering the event, he showed me a house on the school grounds where the priests once lived. He told me I could use the kitchen in that house to prepare for my function. "How can I repay you," I asked him. He smiled kindly and said, "You already did. With tamales."

I then became inspired to turn my passion into a catering business, which I named Pica-di-yo, a traditional Mexican dish and a Spanish play on words. Completely enthused, I immediately went on to cater the Art Fair in Clayton, Missouri, an event attended by 150,000, and successfully fed thousands. I began to see that I needed to say "yes" more often!

Next, I set my sights on the "Taste of St. Louis." For months, I had been badgering the director of the event to let me participate. He told me my business needed to be an LLC, and I was a caterer, not a restaurant. My persistence finally paid off and they accepted my newly registered LLC catering business to the "Taste of St. Louis." There, Pica-di-yo served more than 1,000 empanadas, churros, and tacos to 250,000 people. We even outsold the other two main Mexican restaurants and were voted "Best Churro!" After that, orders rolled in. I started teaching cooking classes and sharing my cultural secrets. I was on an exciting ride and ready for anything!

DARK DAYS

Even though business was great, life was not perfect. Back in 2010, I had a hysterectomy. For most women, this is a standard operation, but for me, I fought a raging bladder infection for the next three years. We tried every antibiotic, but nothing worked. I became depressed and soothed myself by overeating. I gained weight and received a diagnosis of borderline diabetes and high cholesterol.

I began to miss Mexico even more. I missed the warm, constant sunshine which reminded me that no matter how bad things got, the sun would rise each day, and everything would be okay. Without it, life felt dreary. I remember waking up in the mornings thinking, "Yay, I survived another day." That's all I expected out of life anymore—to survive. I immersed myself in taking care of others. Everyone mattered except me. I withdrew from everything and didn't go anywhere, using my kids as an excuse to stay home.

Then, one day, a friend showed up at my door and said, "Enough is enough, no?" She made me take a walk with her, but I could only walk for 10 minutes. Anytime I tried to do it alone, I ended up calling my husband to come and get me. It was so hard to take these small steps towards regaining the life I had lost, not only because of my physical limitations, but because of my depression too. I decided to pray the rosary while I walked, offering up the unpleasant exercise to someone else, because I certainly didn't feel like doing it for myself.

One day I was on the treadmill at the gym, when I suddenly dropped my rosary. Picking it up, I bumped my phone, and it skipped to an upbeat Enrique Iglesias song. Suddenly, I felt like running. I ran for five minutes, and so began my relationship with running. I continued running almost daily and eating healthier, which led to a total 50-pound weight loss! Exercise became my medication for depression. People complimented me on the weight loss, but I had the feeling that the transformation I was undergoing was more than just physical. It was preparing me for something bigger. I could feel the sun coming out, and I knew it was going to make everything better.

TEQUILA!

Continuing with my business, the more I learned about food, the more I became interested in learning about pairing food with drinks. I quickly realized that my clients would ask me about tequila more than any other beverage. When I started reading more about the tequila-making process, it piqued my curiosity, and I decided to travel to Mexico to learn more.

Tequila, the most emblematic Mexican drink, has an interesting manufacturing process. Most people are amazed to learn that the tequila they hold in their hands is at least seven years in the making. The best tequilas are made with 100 percent Blue Agave Tequilana Weber, a plant which takes seven or eight years to grow to maturity in Mexico. From there, the *jima* (harvest), processing, and fermentation are all multi-step processes. I find it fascinating and am passionate about explaining it to people. There are different types of tequila, and their properties can be explained by the type of barrel used and how long each tequila was aged inside. This results in the tequilas having varying colors, smells, and infused notes.

I started offering tequila tastings as a sensory experience, where the group tastes, smells, and feels both the tequila and agave as they learn about the tequila-making process. I appeal to their imagination as I share the long journey of the agave to become the beautiful liquid they hold in their hands. I ask them to try to distinguish different aromas, such as vanilla, butter, and lavender, among others. I had finally found the bridge between my American and Mexican self. Tequila called me home, as it helped me connect with my neighbors and retain my Mexican roots.

During a trip to Mexico, I was delayed for eleven hours in the Houston airport. There, I noticed an elegantly dressed gentleman in his eighties, and I decided to walk over and introduce myself. We began to converse, and I told him about my interest in tequila. Mentioning he was involved in the tequila industry, he opened his wallet to give me his business card. The man's name was Don Jaime Orendain, and he was the owner of Tequila Orendain, one of the oldest tequila distilleries in Mexico. Don Jaime arranged a tour of the distillery for me. I knew I needed to follow my passion. So, I did.

After that, I decided to find out more about the actual

barrels used in making tequila. Another brand of tequila owned by Don Jaime's sons was on the hunt for American oak barrels, the same kind used by the bourbon manufacturers in the U.S. I didn't know anything about bourbon except that it came from Kentucky. Determined to find the barrels, I hatched a plan to take my kids on a weekend trip to Kentucky. After several placing several calls from the hotel, I finally found a "cooperage" that made the barrels that the distillery wanted. I was able to negotiate a deal selling barrels to the distillery in Mexico. It was a win for everyone involved.

When you chase your dreams, magic happens. I reinvented myself and took my life and my business in a completely different direction. It felt right. Meeting Don Jaime opened doors to the tequila industry, which has embraced me and provided so many opportunities to share my heritage. Now, I can't wait to wake up and start a new day. My love for learning about tequila and sharing it with others energizes me because I am able to share a piece of Mexico and a piece of myself.

Today, I'm expanding my love for Mexican spirits by becoming an expert in all agave spirits, including Tequila, Mezcal, and Raicilla. I'm also planning group experiences to distilleries in Mexico, and my catering and tequila tasting businesses are thriving. My faith continues to guide me in business and life, and I'm happy and healthy because I have found what I am called to do. I'm proud that it's a pursuit that connects two beautiful countries, both entwined within my heart. Now the sun is out, and Mexico is with me always!

REFLECTION QUESTIONS

1. Have you ever been in a situation where you didn't fit in? What did you do?

2. What do you do for yourself that can be considered "self-care?"

3. What can you do today to help pursue your passion?

BIOGRAPHY

Born and raised in Mexico City, MariCarmen Ortiz-Conway earned a bachelor's degree in communication in 1989, and later moved to St. Louis in 1992 to be with her husband. She and her husband raised four boys, who are the center of her life. In 2015, she founded Pica-di-yo, now a well-known catering company in St. Louis, Missouri. MariCarmen has an unstoppable passion for her roots and the perseverance to reach her dreams for her family.

Missing the flavors, smells, textures, and culture of her Mexican heritage when she moved to the United States, MariCarmen learned to keep her roots alive through the art of cooking and sharing her culture with others. She now caters many local events, including the St. Louis Art Fair. She was one of the only catering companies originally selected to serve the Taste of St. Louis event, which is attended annually by 250,000 people. MariCarmen also teaches cooking classes and is a certified tequila expert who will soon offer tastings on Mezcal and Raicilla as well.

MariCarmen believes nothing is impossible and is ever grateful for how the universe keeps putting things in her path through "coincidences" to keep her growing stronger in her business and personal life.

MariCarmen Ortiz-Conway
picadiyoll@gmail.com
Facebook: Pica-di-yo

Lisba Romo

"The more you embrace discomfort, the braver and more fearless you become."

I was born on the north side of Chicago. At two years old, my parents moved me to what I called the "sandwich," in the middle of Pilsen and Little Village, two predominantly Mexican neighborhoods on the southwest side of Chicago.

In my early years, I would find happiness playing outside from morning until evening. I remember my mom yelling out the window that it was time to come in. I spent most of my summer days riding my bicycle. Yet on a regular school day, I was a shy, depressed kid full of fear and low self-esteem. I was bullied at school and too shy to speak up for myself. I vividly remember coming to pick up my second-grade report card and hearing my teacher tell my mom that sometimes she didn't even know I was in the classroom. That comment stuck in my mind. I thought to myself, if the teacher doesn't even know I'm here, I must not be that important.

On one occasion, I recall crying in front of class. One teacher that would forever impact my life told me, "Lisba, stop crying. Lift up your head! Look at me!" He would give me the motivation I needed and push me out of my comfort zone.

He had the entire class rehearse a song that would later become our school anthem. In front of everyone, he said, "See how Lisba is singing? That is how it should be done!" No one else could do it like me. I felt special. That teacher continued to push me and encourage me every chance he could, and I noticed God begin to place people in my life that would help me.

FACING BULLIES

However, I was being bullied both at school and home. One day, I stood up to a group of school bullies and told them they had better stop messing with me or I would kick their ^%$! It worked for a while, but before it got better, it got worse. There was a girl who kept on pushing and bothering me until I was fed up and started fighting her. I had so much built-up anger and was so blinded with rage, I ended up on top of her as she lay on her stomach on the ground. I sat on her back, punching her continuously on the head until she started yelling, "Okay, stop, stop already, I won't mess with you!" Someone had to pull me off of her. I cannot lie. It all made me feel a lot better because I had released what I was feeling inside.

At home, I was verbally abused by my mom. I felt I never measured up to her standards, and she would often yell and curse at me. She felt I had to do things her way, because her way was better. However, there was voice in my head that sometimes told me that I would be someone important one day. I don't know how, but I knew God was speaking to me.

I also remember having great childhood memories which

were my escapes every summer break. The best moments were when my dad would drive all of us to Texas and Mexico to visit our families. I remember singing songs and sharing different stories together throughout our road trip. I would spend endless days of laughter and fun with my cousins, aunts, uncles, and my beloved *"Buelita,"* my grandma from Texas. During these vacations I felt I could just be myself. Little did I know that those summer breaks with my *Buelita* would have such a positive influence in my life.

My *Buelita* always had something great to say about me. She would tell me I'm a precious jewel, that I'm beautiful, that I'm so special and smart. God was using my *Buelita* to build up my self-esteem. It was as if she knew I needed to hear her words! As I grew older, things got better, but then again, life had some challenges for me.

When I was in high school, I went to bed one night with my sister, who shared our bed, when I was spiritually attacked by an evil force and I heard a whispering voice, talking very quickly. "Get up! Go to the pantry and do drugs! I'll tell you what to get from there, just go!" it said. There was a buzzing sound, as if there was a fly buzzing over my ear. I looked up and there wasn't anything there. My sister was fast asleep.

I remember walking to the pantry and looking at it and then waking up my parents just to hear them speak. I went back to sleep and the voices continued, so I started praying non-stop, asking for God to help me. I prayed until the voice went away. God was there for me again.

In high school, I remember having suicidal thoughts. I remember needing to pray every time I had these thoughts. I never shared this with anyone because I thought they would think I was crazy. When I graduated from high school, I promised myself I would make my college years better.

CHALLENGES AND REDEMPTION

As soon as I started college, I did exactly that. I started to leave my comfort zone. I did things to challenge myself and get uncomfortable. I would stand up for others, and do things other people wouldn't do. I started singing at school and local restaurants. I started writing and joined the school newspaper. I became a student ambassador and started traveling to other countries. As I got more uncomfortable, something magical started to happen. I became stronger. Then I met a great friend who brought me closer to Jesus Christ and I accepted Him as my Lord and Savior.

Three months later, I landed my first job at a mortgage company. I was so excited. Little did I know that shortly after starting, the leadership would show their true colors. I discovered they were all chauvinistic men, except for my supervisor, who was a female. Soon they made her uncomfortable, too, which encouraged her to quit.

I knew I had to be strong and stay to get my work experience. They promoted me. I started helping with their marketing efforts, however the work environment was still toxic. I overlooked the negatives, but deep inside I was getting depressed because I would wake up every morning to a job I hated.

I remember crying at times after work with the man who is now my husband. He would push me to become stronger. I remember listening to anything and anyone that would give me motivation. I played CDs from Joel Osteen, a pastor at a Mega Church, over and over again. God was speaking to me through those recordings.

Then the day came when I was laid off from my job. I remember the CEO's son telling me they no longer needed my position and that it was my last day. I cried as I left the office and co-workers told me I would find something better.

God showed up again and gave me a better job, which would be the total opposite work environment of the last one. I now had a positive working environment where I felt valued. I started off as a receptionist and got promoted up to marketing manager. I grew fond of my co-workers and built great relationships there. Then it happened again.

I was called into a meeting with the CEO and told that I would never, ever become a marketing director within the company and that day would be my last day. I couldn't believe this was happening again, and I couldn't believe that someone I cared for would say something like this to me. I cried again as I walked out of the office, feeling underestimated.

I knew that what was ahead of me would not be an easy road. Back then, I dedicated most of my free time to serving as a youth director for a nonprofit organization that helped girls, ages 12-18, develop their leadership skills through a program I co-developed. I also partnered with an organization that helped me learn how money works, which helped me tremendously. Both helped me bring in some income, however my finances were not good. I remember almost losing my house and my car and not having enough income to pay for basic things. Eventually, I had to file for bankruptcy.

I remember going to teach the workshops with my girls when I had a negative balance in my checking account. I promised myself I would not let them down like I had been let down before. Their smiling faces and the positive changes I saw in them helped me to stay strong until my girls completed their program.

Then, my dad was diagnosed with stage four colon cancer, and I helped my family take care of him. I couldn't hold a full-time job, and instead did temp jobs so I could spend time with dad, whose health was declining each day. My dad's sickness, along with the struggle of our finances, is what kept me in constant worry. I remember fighting with my husband about our finances. I didn't know it yet, but I was developing anxiety.

One day, I found myself having a full-blown panic attack. I felt like I was having a heart attack. I started praying non-stop, and it helped me calm down. My health was declining too. One morning, I woke up and realized the left side of my face was paralyzed. I was freaking out! I went to the hospital and they diagnosed it as Bell's Palsy. I knew I had to make some changes in my life because I would have constant anxiety, which caused my tension headaches. My smile wasn't the same. I remember thinking I would never look the same way again. It was a challenging time for me. I started taking supplements, going for facial therapy, and doing anything that would help me. I wasn't going to give up until I got better.

BEING BRAVE

Then what we feared the most happened. My dad passed away and the loss rocked me to my core. I was close to my dad. He came to the U.S. with nothing and had achieved so much in a country that was foreign to him. He had been two years away from retiring and living his lifelong dream of going back to Mexico. Instead, he had lost the battle against cancer.

My dad had to hold off on his dream. I promised myself that I would be brave with my life, and that I would not hold back. I promised myself I would continue his legacy. Something sparked in me. I started doing what I knew would help me. I started getting out of my comfort zone. I launched the "Be Brave and Get Uncomfortable Challenge," where for 10 days I tried to do things I felt uncomfortable doing. I found that the more you embrace discomfort, the more brave and fearless you become.

I also had a one-on-one conversation with my mom, where I told her how she had affected me, and we both cried together and hugged each other. "I was only trying to help in my own way. I love you," she told me. All was forgiven.

I started building a new organization called "Be Brave. Be You." to help other women and girls confront their fears and live the best version of themselves. I realized how God was present throughout the entire time, and how He continues to show up in my life.

I would like to dedicate this story to my husband, my mom, my two sisters, my brother, my father, grandmother Elvira, my favorite teacher, Dana Butler, and to all my family and friends who have believed in me and continue to support me in my mission. I also thank God for the struggles, because they made me stronger and the woman I am today.

REFLECTION QUESTIONS

1. What fears are holding you back?

2. What things are you doing to help you grow, even if they are uncomfortable?

3. Who have you not forgiven?

BIOGRAPHY

Lisba Romo is a passionate, driven Latina community advocate leader who loves to empower and help others to be brave with their lives so that they can fulfill the lives they are designed to live. She launched an organization called "Be Brave. Be You," to empower women and girls of all ages through motivational speaking, leadership workshops, and her "Be Brave. Be You" YouTube channel, where she interviews women and girls who have confronted their fears, gotten uncomfortable and become real-life heroes or "Brave SHERO."

Lisba partners with a financial nonprofit organization which teaches financial literacy out in the community. Lisba is also a Home Care Supervisor for a large nonprofit organization that assists the elderly with their daily living activities within their homes. She currently resides in the southwest side of Chicago with her husband and doggy, named "Foxy."

Lisba Romo
bebravebyou@gmail.com
https://bebravebyou.com/

Patricia del Rosario Hernandez Figueroa

"The more I give, the more I receive."

Tell your story to other women, Latinas or other nationalities, immigrants, or natives, so they don't repeat your mistakes and, instead, learn from your experiences. If only one of them benefits from hearing about your journey to where you are now, your story was worth telling... so here goes mine.

CHANGES IN CHICAGO

December 2000 was cold and blustery when I arrived in Chicago. I was greeted by what I felt was the most unbearable cold of my life as I struggled to come to terms with a new place and definitively put the toxic, abusive relationship with my first son's father behind me. Arriving in Chicago was also full of emotions associated with walking into something new, both for me and for little *Pecokin*, the name I affectionately call my older son, Julio Cesar. The plan was to stay for six months, which was the length of my visa. I was going to live the adventure, work as much as possible, purchase a car, and then return to my home country where I worked in the House of Representatives of the State of Mexico when my visa expired. Also, I was going to meet one of my brothers who I hadn't seen in twelve years, and, yes, you guessed it--love also played a role, as I was about to reunite with the love of my teenage years, and the love of my life, Roy.

I was also feeling many raw emotions, right under my skin. It was sad leaving my beautiful country, my customs, my mother, my family, and friends... yes, it was a lot. From my initial stay to what eventually became 20 years, I am, and always will be, thankful for all this country has given me, and also for everything it has taken away from me.

I think that somewhere we have our fate written down so we can follow through on it. My decision to stay here was an emotional one. When it was time to return to Mexico and my government job, I was presented with an engagement ring from Roy. I cancelled the plane tickets for us to return to Mexico. I knew my visa was expiring and my position in Mexico would no longer wait for me if I stayed. Yet, I exchanged my job of 12 years for the unknown with someone I loved.

Anyway, it was done. I started my first job as a waitress in the U.S., with the help of my siblings Nora and Rene, and the guidance of my brother-in-law, Fidel. I wasn't afraid of working anywhere, in any position, because, thanks be given to God, my mother taught us to work hard since we were kids. It didn't matter to me that I was exchanging a well-cut suit for a waitress apron. I had something to do, I could do it, and I was happy I even had a job. It helped that I was determined to do my best, and that I had the blessing of having good people who helped me get on my feet. Thank you, Marisol, my manager, for this and more.

Life went on, with more jobs. I went from waitress to busgirl, cashier, store manager, limousine chauffeur, manager of a business that send parcels and transfers to Latin American countries, dance instructor, teacher's assistant in charge of incredible kids... the list goes on and on. There were, of course, good experiences, and not-so-good ones. Sadly enough, it wasn't easy working with Latino workmates and customers. The exact same ones I expected to be more sympathetic were rude, and sometimes even abusive, but that's another story. I met many different people, learned about the different cultures in global Chicago. I heard many stories, always thinking that mine was the saddest one, just to realize that there is always somebody with a sadder, more tragic experience, and so I developed a strong sense of compassion and sympathy for people who were belittled, abused, and mistreated as I was in my own time.

I think fighting injustice has always been very much part of my personality, so I was ready to continue fighting for those who didn't have a voice. There were times in my past, particularly when I lived and worked in Alabama, when I noticed the undocumented restaurant staff was being treated unfairly with a permanent threat of being laid off if we displeased the management in any way. We weren't even allowed to take breaks between duties. Complaints, if any, were almost always followed by dismissal.

I had my own problems now, though. Once my permit expired I became increasingly afraid to speak up for myself, even though it was critical that I remain in the U.S. I was with Roy, but I still needed the resources to be responsible for my son and pay the mortgage bills from Mexico that were still coming in. I recall thanking God in my prayers for every day and every night at bedtime, asking not to be found by immigration agents, and most of all, to never be separated from my son.

Julio was having a hard time, too. It was almost impossible to keep him away from the bad things that were happening in school, and to make things worse, he experienced abuse from teachers and principals when he was in first grade in Alabama. Many years thereafter, he found courage to talk about it, and I finally understood that the reason he never told me was because he assumed I would be ok with how he was disciplined. From that terrible experience, I learned that we must be open with our children, so they never think that we aren't there for them when they need us.

Not everything was bad, though. I had Roy; however, it didn't last long, because one day he left me without saying a word. There was no villain; it's always a matter of two. But it was devastating to feel all alone again, like I had failed one more time, and I may not have a future at all.

The only one who lifted my spirits was my then 10-year-old son, lying in bed at my side, when he said, "Mom, don't cry, I know that God brought me to this world so I could hug you when you're going through this." When I heard him saying what he said, I realized that I was being selfish, thinking only of my own misfortunes, without understanding that the true reason why I should stand up one more time was right there staring at me. I can't tell you how miserable I felt… but it was time to start again.

STARTING OVER

I told my son that we were ready for a new beginning. I asked for his forgiveness, and reminded him of two quotes that have been with me in my bad times: *"The harder you fall, the stronger you'll rise,"* and *"If God is holding your hand, nothing will stand in your way."* Looking back, I'm thankful for having had such a great partner in my son Julio when I needed one the most, and also because I was able to forgive myself, turn the page for the best, and to decide, once and forever, that I was to do whatever it would take to move on.

There was no old-way Patricia any longer. As I reflect on those years, the only explanation of how I was able to fight off depression and get back on my feet is that I found a purpose for my life, refused to be angry or vengeful, and turned my energy into doing new things without feeling envy, or hurting anyone. It was time to restart my education, to take decisions to improve my life, and my son's, and to start thinking about having my own business, a dream that perhaps had waited for too long.

I made my $535, biweekly check stretch enough to eat, dress, pay for our needs, and even shop secondhand. At that time, I also started driving a limousine to the airport and sparing weekends to teach dance to a *quinceañera* so I could save some money to purchase toys and books. I was intending to start a childcare business, and I named it "The Magic Castle." That was the name of my first classroom as an early childhood education assistant teacher, so I felt it was the perfect name for my new business. I've now had it for more than eleven years.

Thank you, God, because of the many blessings you've given to somebody who doesn't even speak the language of this country very well. Thank you, my dear mother, Juany... your love has always been unconditional, and you have always been at my side. Thank you, brother Rene, for giving me a place to live and the limousine trips that helped so much, and also for letting me start my first business in your home. I had my love life wonderfully blessed with the return of my husband and the arrival of our beloved, and much-desired son, with all he meant, and will always mean to me. Thank you, Roy, my son Julio, my niece Estefany, and my loyal assistant Miriam... because none of what happened, and is still happening, would have been possible without you all.

Everyone can see the results, and so can I. There was a point in my life when things turned for the better, and then continued on to become the best. Once I was professionally grown and emotionally stable, all blessings seemed to fall on me at the same time.

Even better, my blessings have never ended by the grace of God. Now, my husband and I keep fighting for our dreams, because the triumph is in the fight. Whenever we arrive at the finish line, we're ready to start anew. We keep expanding our business and our horizons, helping as many people as we possibly can, with no interest other than seeing others flourish as we have.

THE FIGHT AND THE FLOW

If there is something I've learned, it's that the more I give, the more I receive, and that when you help others selflessly, many more opportunities come your way. As my dear friend Jackie says, one grows step by step, and it's only at a certain point when all the magic in you simply flows. When I learned what a boomerang was, I realized that everything you do comes back eventually, both the good and the bad. Isn't it true? Dreams lead to promises, and a promise that comes true is what we all hope to achieve.

I know my story is similar to that of many Latinas, although each one of us faces adversity in a different, unique way. Dear friends, don't think you're ready to fight your battle, because most likely you aren't. The key is to fight with what you've got: your faith, your dear ones, your dreams…you name it. The best thing that I'm sure will happen to you, as it happened to me, is to learn that you're capable of forgiving, moving forward, and standing up again, over and over, as long as there is a reason for you to go on. I have mine, and it's giving to others. Do you have yours?

REFLECTION QUESTIONS

1. Have you ever had to start all over in life? If so, how do you reflect on it, now that it is all in the past?

2. What painful experience has brought out the best in you?

3. My loved ones made me who I am. How do you reward your loved ones for all the good deeds they do?

BIOGRAPHY

Patricia del Rosario Hernandez Figueroa was born in Puebla, Mexico, to a single mother. She lived in Toluca, Mexico, briefly, then moved to Chicago 20 years ago. What started as a short stay quickly turned into "forever."

Patricia is the youngest of six siblings and has been married for 17 years to the love of her life. She is the proud mother of two, and received a degree in early childhood education from St. Augustine College. She then moved on to create new opportunities, which she does well. She opened her restaurant, El Agave Mexican Grill, and operates the Magic Castle, a childcare center. With her family, she opened additional locations known as The Magic Forest, The Magic Kingdom, and The Magic Place. There she teaches and cares for her little treasures and looks forward to more ventures.

Inspired by her realization that the parents of the children she cares for have many unmet needs, Patricia launched a project called "Fusión Latina Chicago." The organization functions as a help center for Latinas to find answers to difficult questions, from how to start a business to how to file a police report, or start a nonprofit. She also conducted *"Entre Nosotras,"* an online radio reality show.

Patricia del Rosario Hernández Figueroa
phernandez@fusionlatinachicago.com
(312) 287 8166
www.fusionlatinachicago.com

Nancy Scovotti

"Believe in yourself and always dare to dream."

Over dinner last night, my mom shared a family tradition I did not know existed. She and her siblings were all named after the "Saint of the Day" when they were born. Luckily, we did not continue the tradition because I would have been named Margaret, and my daughter would have been named Maria Gabriela. Although, in my eyes, the tradition suits my mother perfectly because she is a saint.

At bedtime I tucked in my daughter and felt inclined to share with her that as a little girl I was not a dreamer, something only my inner circle knows. I proceeded to tell her that I was afraid to dream because if my dreams did not come true, I would feel I failed. After the words came out of my mouth, I felt immediate regret. How could I possibly share this with my daughter and potentially pass on my fears to her? As a mother, I need to be a role model and lead by example. However, at that very moment, something amazing happened. I felt a sudden rush throughout my body. It was as if I released that fear out into the universe and it was no longer part of my being.

The next day when I arrived home, I walked into a

painted canvas from my daughter that read DREAM in the front. In the back, was a note...

'19 Reimagined

To Margaret-

Dreams know the way. And, if they hit rock bottom, the only way to go is up into the stars. Never be afraid to dream the things you could never imagine.

-Maria Gabriela

Life is complete...

AMERICAN DREAM

I am a "Chicana," born in Chicago from 100 percent Mexican parents. I was raised by my single *mami* who worked two jobs. I vividly remember the bright bedroom lights on my face every morning while she helped me get dressed to go to daycare, while it was still dark outside, so she could go to her first job. After daycare I would go to the babysitter, and she picked me up when it was dark again, after her second shift. Although we had humble beginnings, somehow she managed to give my two brothers and I an abundance of love in our home (love is her secret). Due to limited means and mindset, achieving the "American Dream" of owning a home was never a thought.

Eighteen years ago, as a young newly engaged couple, my husband suggested we buy a condominium and my natural response was, "Why not rent?" I was living with my mom and she was renting; that's all I knew. Ironically, I had all the contacts at my fingertips; I just did not know enough to even ask.

A few days later my boss randomly mentioned there was a foreclosed condominium unit I should see and consider buying and my natural response was, "sure." He was my boss, so of course I said yes. Then I thought back to one of Richard Branson's quotes... *"If somebody offers you an amazing opportunity but you are not sure you can do it, say YES - then learn how to do it later!"* At that time, I did not realize it was a great opportunity and how it was going to impact my future!

Our next step was finding out if we qualified for a mortgage. Being in the title insurance industry, I already had connections, and sure enough I got the quick answer that it was cheaper to buy than rent. Wow, that was an eye opener!

After learning the buying process and determining our price range, we submitted our offer for the condo, but sadly enough, we were outbid. However, buying was now our only option because we were determined to become homeowners. Shortly thereafter, we purchased our very first condo unit. Five years later, we sold it, and doubled our investment. With that, we had our down payment to buy the home we live in now with our kids, in a fantastic school district. Had we rented, we would have had nothing to put towards our purchase.

Fortunately, I was surrounded by people who encouraged and influenced me to have more. My husband always thinks BIG, and my manager walked the walk and talked the talk. I knew following his footsteps would lead us in the right direction.

As I get older, engage in deeper conversations, and roll in different circles (I call it diversifying), it becomes blatantly obvious that who you surround yourself with truly matters. Be protective of your energy and who you spend most of your time with; it makes a huge difference.

After feeling depleted, I started writing in my gratitude journal. It was a game changer. I learned to become a better listener and be present for those who are important in my life. There is so much to be grateful for, yet many of us focus on what is going wrong. I invite you to self-evaluate who is in your immediate circle and, most importantly, make changes if necessary. Not everyone wants to see you win, and those are not your people. Do not grandfather people in; they do not deserve so much of your attention, even if they are your family. Keep your time limited with those you know you can't realistically remove from your life and try to find the good in them. I know it's hard; I have been there. Dig deep. There is something good in all of us.

BE. DO. HAVE.

Sometimes others see the potential and greatness within you when you don't see it yourself. Those are the people you want to surround yourself with, and in due time you get to pay it forward. Gifts are made to be given; the more you learn, the more you have to offer.

Throughout my entire adult life, I have hired coaches in various areas: business, life, nutrition, and, most recently, public speaking. Seek out mentors, coaches, gurus, accountability partners, etc. Welcome support, guidance, and constructive criticism as long as your source has your best interest at heart. We don't wake up with confidence, especially of the unknown. Others may have experience in what you would like to achieve. I look at it like having a fast pass to get to your goal quicker and free you up to pursue the next one.

I have learned to get comfortable with the uncomfortable; that is the only way to continuously grow and improve every day. I open myself up to feedback from my close circle. I ask them, "What am I doing right, and what can I do better?" This has helped me to celebrate my wins and to be less judgmental (and softer too). It's all still a work in progress.

In addition, serving on various organizations and different boards has helped me develop a valuable skill that effectively identifies people's strengths, and creates winning teams. Being surrounded by amazing leaders, and women that look like me and are achieving massive success, lights a fire in my belly. I dare to have the audacity to dream that I can do it, too. *Si se puede!* (Yes, you can!)

Always invest in YOUrself. I firmly believe it is the best investment you can make. We come into this world without an instruction manual, roadmap, or blueprint...more like a blank canvas, and we need to mindfully create our very own masterpiece.

Having a BE. DO. HAVE. attitude has helped me in the last few years. Know who you have to be, determine what you need to do, and your actions will deliver what you want to have. The secret is in the being... always be a *Chingona* (badass)!

NANCY'S "TO BE" AND "DON'T" LISTS

1. BE SELECTIVE. Surround yourself with people who add value to your life as you do to theirs. Seek like-minded people with similar goals and a good heart, who are good at and enjoy doing things you do not do well. Create a win-win by tapping into each other's strengths. Together we can achieve more.

2. BE PRESENT. Really listen and give people your undivided attention, preferably without your cell phone in sight. If possible, leave it in your car!

3. BE INTENTIONAL. Walk in with at least one goal in mind; it will increase your odds of winning.

4. BE KIND. It's good for your soul and can make a world of a difference in someone else's life.

5. BE HONEST. Speak your truth. Some people may not like it, but you can agree to disagree. If not, accept that some people may not like you and just know they probably don't like themselves either.

6. BE GRATEFUL. A grateful heart is always full. Journal at night. When you mindfully recap your day, you'll be amazed at how blessed you really are.

7. BE AUTHENTIC. Being you is your POWER! Be the energy you wish to receive. Light up the room by simply being you!

I learned to use what others would see as limited beliefs to my advantage, and as gifts. Even though I was not a big dreamer growing up, I always knew what I did NOT want. Here is a list of some tried-and-true behaviors you SHOULD AVOID in order to keep focused on your dreams. Please DON'T:

1. PUT YOURSELF LAST. Self-care is instrumental to your success. Schedule "me" time to do more of what makes YOU happy.

2. FORGET TO HAVE FUN. Schedule it if you have to; it takes practice. Add it to your calendar as an appointment.

3. ACT LIKE A VICTIM. There is always a way to dig yourself out. Focus on the end result you desire and trust the process.

4. SURROUND YOURSELF WITH NEGATIVE PEOPLE. Their toxicity will stunt your growth. *Mejor sola que mal acompañada* (Better alone than in bad company).

5. TRY TO MAKE EVERYONE HAPPY. It's an inside job, and not yours!

6. OVERTHINK THINGS. Procrastination will weigh you down and you could miss good opportunities.

7. EXPECT EVERYONE TO HAVE YOUR WORK ETHIC OR MORALS. They are not YOU!

NOTE: Living a happy life takes intention, purpose, and practice.

LOVE ABOVE ALL

My *mami* has loved me unconditionally with every step I have taken. Simply knowing I have her by my side keeps me going; she is my secret weapon. My husband has always believed in me, even when I doubted myself. He continues to be my biggest fan. Together we are mindful of how we raise our children, to make sure they feel loved and know we will always be there to cheer them on. We are blessed with our daughter, Isabella, who is smart like her momma and competitively sporty like her *papi*. Our son, Daniel, is an undercover genius, enjoys math problem solving, and has recently embraced meditating in his school classroom.

With all that said, I must share with you my most recent self-discovery. In life, knowing how to love YOUrself and being happy in your own skin is the secret. Find what makes you happy, what fuels your soul, and do more of that. Truly own who you are, love yourself, and live your true life unapologetically!

Stop waiting for the perfect day; it may never come. Just let the magic begin. Trust your gut and let your instincts guide you, because deep down inside, we all know the answer. As I look back, I realize I did not take enough risks in the past. I now realize the reason for that was my fear of failure. Identify the self-limitations and beliefs you created, then break the cycle and it will set you free.

Cheers to you living your best life ever. Whatever you begin, believe in yourself and always dare to dream.

Lastly, enjoy these words of wisdom in tribute to my life coach, Deborah Nelson Shimer, who lived life to the fullest: "Live your best f***** life because YOU can!"

REFLECTION QUESTIONS

1. Do your dreams scare you? If not, they are not big enough. Take time to re-evaluate.

2. Who do you have to BEcome to attract what you desire? Be. Do. Have.

3. Are you living a purposeful and intentional life that represents the best version of YOU?

BIOGRAPHY

Nancy Scovotti was born in Chicago, Illinois. She and her two brothers were raised by a single, hard-working Mexican mother. More than thirty years ago, she moved to New York, where she lives with her husband Danny, and their two children, Isabella and Daniel. She is a feisty *"Chingona,"* unapologetically living her best life, on her terms, while staying true to herself.

Nancy is an industry-recognized, top title insurance sales executive and senior vice president with The Great American Title Agency, Inc. She has earned her reputation in the real estate community for her efficiency and commitment to customer service as a matter of principle. Nancy has more than 24 years of experience developing strong relationships, connecting industry professionals, and mindfully creating a win-win for all. She offers an unparalleled closing experience by using a no-stone-unturned approach.

In a continuous state of self-development and growth, Nancy co-founded INSPIRA, a mastermind group that inspires individuals looking to grow and work together toward becoming the best versions of themselves. She is committed to building a community of like-minded individuals willing to collaborate and add value to others. She realizes the POWER of mentorship, accountability, and execution in order to find success.

Nancy Scovotti
NScovotti@gmail.com
(914) 841-622

Monika Alvarez

*"Once you are clear about your desires, God and the universe
will conspire in your favor."*

Every woman has the opportunity to live a life full of abundance and happiness, but very few women know that the power to have it all lies within themselves. I believe you, too, can uncover a life of fulfillment, harmony, and happiness with yourself and everything around you. If you learn to balance your life in certain areas, you can be connected with abundance and have everything you ever wanted. Even if you face adversity, if you follow what I am about to share with you, you will be able to overcome your challenges with creativity.

I think a balanced life starts with knowing exactly what lifestyle you want. Don't rush into answering this question. Take time to reflect on your life; where have you been, where are you today and most importantly, where do you wish to be. All of the answers lie within you, and everything starts with you.

You need to know yourself very well. What are your talents? What do you like and dislike? What makes you happy? What makes you feel thrilled and motivated to take action? Once you have answers to these questions, your destiny will become clear.

Life is very simple, but unfortunately, we tend to complicate it at times.

I know you were programmed to think and act a certain way based on your upbringing. However, you have also probably come across situations and people and ask yourself: "Why can't I have that lifestyle? Why can't I travel like other women do? Why can't I enjoy everything she does?" And the answer is, you can, and you absolutely deserve it, too! All of that and much more!

All you need to do is define what you desire most in life. Sounds easy, right? Well, I can assure you, it is!

If you are ready to become the best version of yourself, this story is for you.

THE ANSWERS

I was part of corporate America, had an incredible job, was traveling around the world, earning six figures, and everything was wonderful, according to my terms. Then I turned 40 and everything started to change. I started feeling stuck in life, confused, and worst of all, very empty. So, I decided to put a stop to my professional career, to find myself, and, most importantly, to discover my happiness.

I thought to myself, I can have all the time in the world to do the things I enjoy most: attend family gatherings, spend time with my boys and my husband, and do things that I always had put aside because of work. However, I was not ready for the dramatic lifestyle change. As an executive, I was always on the go, attached to my phone, serving my clients, always in meetings, and motivated by a monthly sales quota that I could share with my boss. Now, I would be at peace and enjoy being a stay-at-home mom.

The first three months were amazing. I slept in, had long coffee chats with friends, and shopped whenever I wanted, as long as I wanted. I lounged around the house without make-up, attended weekend parties with family and friends, and completed day-to-day chores, but after three months I was done. I realized I was not born to be Cinderella. I needed to do something as soon as possible or I would die inside instead of living a fulfilled and happy life.

So, I entered a discovery phase. I started asking myself over and over 'what do I need to do to be happy?' I thought the answer would be in other people and other activities, but it was not. None of them fulfilled my expectations. Thanks to my stubbornness and curiosity, I concluded that every human being has a mission in life, and I was determined to find mine. Once you are clear about your desires, God and the universe will conspire in your favor to provide the resources and the people to make them a reality.

So, in February of 2015, I was invited to my first women entrepreneur meeting. Later, I realized it was the universe sending me my first sign to connect with my mission in life. My adventure as a woman entrepreneur started that day. At the meeting, I was surrounded by happy, vibrant women, with a high level of enthusiasm for life and an incredible positive energy. I said to myself, 'I want to feel the same way; I want to be part of that.'

The meeting was to present a skin care product, but, in reality, that meeting was there to present me a new destiny in life. I left the meeting feeling wonderful, and to my surprise, I ended up falling in love with the skin care product. Most importantly, I was thrilled to know I had a huge potential to introduce this product internationally. Having 20 plus years of experience in international sales, I was sure I could sell the product everywhere it could be sold. I was certain this was a great opportunity, and the right time for me to become an entrepreneur.

I started visualizing everything I desired. I established goals and allowed myself to dream again. I decided I was not going to limit myself, and my adventure as an entrepreneur began. I started working from home while implementing all of my executive woman skills.

It was a wonderful season in my life. I was surrounded with incredible, highly energetic people, and a community of like-minded women who desired more. At some point in their life, they too had experienced moments of confusion and discouragement, just like me, but they were determined to find their answers and had big hopes for their future. So, I realized I had so much more potential that I never developed because I didn't have the courage to do so. I then decided to dive into learning anything and everything about the entrepreneurial world. I read books, attended workshops, conferences, seminars, and more.

A NEW DIRECTION

However, in early December of 2016, even though my goals

had been accomplished by helping the company increase their sales by 75% just in north America, I found myself back in the same place. I was discouraged and had no motivation. Something inside of me was telling me there was more to it, something more powerful. So, I decided to reflect deeply and ask myself the same questions about who I was and where I was going. Once again, the universe answered my questions through my first mentor, Mary Bullard, who taught me how to step into living a life full of abundance.

Having amazing mentors in my life has been the key to my success. I discovered that I could create something unimaginable, something so powerful that it would make my heart happy for the rest of my days. I was able to dream even bigger, but this time my dreams were clearer and more concise.

My life took a 180-degree turn. I realized that if I wanted different results, I had to make changes in my life--changes I had wanted to make for a while, but didn't know where to start or how to establish them. So, I decided to let go of my fear and anything holding me back. It was a daily challenge with constant questions and answers to myself, deep reflections on who I was, what I believed in, what my values were, my culture, and more. All of this helped me find my purpose, and my mission in life.

I can assure you that once you connect with your inner power, you will become unstoppable, but it is very important to know where you are going in life. Once you focus on investing time in learning, growing, and yourself, you will then be able to get everything you've always wanted.

Let's go back to the time where I was anchored, asking myself:

What is my purpose?

What is my mission in life?

Where am I going?

My answers were: I am a wife, a mother, a friend, and an entrepreneur, all combined in one word: Mujer. And how could I combine it all? Through my inner power.

From all these questions and answers and by being fully connected with my inner power, I was able to visualize everything I enjoy today, and that is how *Mujer 6 Dígitos* was born. A platform for women entrepreneurs, where I help them connect with their inner power so they, too, can convert into businesswomen just like me. This inspiration was gained by being surrounded by women who share the same passion for personal and business growth that I have. In order to achieve everything you want, you have to invest time in yourself, and in your unique talents.

THE SIX DIGITS

Mujer 6 Digitos focuses on six fundamental areas of empowerment for women entrepreneurs: health, spirit, profession, mindset, finance, and recreation. The goal is to make the lifestyle you want reality by enjoying the right balance of these areas, and living a fulfilling and happy life by connecting with your inner power.

In order to offer this platform, I need to achieve balance

in myself. So, I continuously invest time, money, and energy in developing myself so I can offer more. I attend strategic conferences and seminars in personal and entrepreneurial growth. I am part of organizations with women entrepreneurs with my same values and vision in life, and I surround myself with great teachers and mentors, one of which is John Maxwell. In 2017, I joined his leadership organization and became certified as a coach, mentor, teacher, and speaker, and now I'm a part of his team.

One thing I did decide from the beginning was that all my services would be offered in Spanish. Even though I am fluent in English, Spanish is my first language, so I feel obligated to commit myself to my Spanish-speaking community, and to all Latinas who need resources in their native language.

The journey has been long and difficult at times, but I have worked tirelessly with enthusiasm and a high level of unshakeable motivation. I like to stay focused and committed to myself, my business, and most importantly, my clients. I am passionate about my purpose and I know there is a mission I need to fulfill. So, with my results I hope to inspire Latinas around the world to take action to establish a balance between their life and businesses, and in the process, I look forward to being part of their transformation!

Today, my responsibility as the founder of *Mujer 6 Digitos,* and as a life and business coach, is to serve entrepreneurs to become businesswomen. I am very proud of myself for achieving a huge milestone in my life and career. My mission is to continue empowering women around the world and to share my knowledge so I can gain their trust by helping them connect to their inner power and strive for anything they can envision. I hope this story can serve you as an inspiration to elevate your life to the next level and to never give up on your dreams.

REFLECTION QUESTIONS

1. How does your life feel, in or out of balance?

2. How would you describe your mission in life?

3. What area in your life has helped you transform yourself, personally or in busines?

BIOGRAPHY

Monika Alvarez was born in Chicago, Illinois, and raised in Aguascalientes, México. Monika is a businesswoman and a life and business coach. She is the founder and CEO of *Mujer 6 Digitos*, an organization for women entrepreneurs which provides personal and professional career-building services focused on business expansion.

A graduate of South Texas College, Monika obtained her associate's degree in business administration. She has more than 20 plus years of experience in international marketing, public relations, sales, communications, finance, event planning, and business development. Her diverse background in sales management has afforded her the opportunity to develop and execute best practices beneficial to owning several businesses and handling the communication for *Club 6 Digitos.*

Monika serves as an active member in a leadership organization worldwide. In her spare time, you will find Monika reading a great book, spending quality time with her family, or traveling overseas. She lives in Mission, Texas, with her husband, Luis Alvarez, and their two sons Miguel Angel Esparza and Luis Alvarez Jr.

Monika Alvarez
Monika@club6digitos.com
+1 (956) 400-9948

Leslie Regalado

"The more I say yes, the more opportunities appear along my journey."

The first life-altering YES in my life took place before I was born. It was my parent's YES to emigrate from Durango, Mexico, to the United States in the late 1970's. I would not have had any of the opportunities I have enjoyed in life if they had not said YES.

When my parents left their country, their hometowns, and their families, they did it to pursue a brighter future for themselves and their future family. I am extremely grateful to them for making that decision and will never be able to repay them. However, I can honor their sacrifice and say YES much more often than no. I can make sure I do not allow fear to paralyze me and hold me back from living the kind of life they wanted for me, or the life I was created to live.

YES, is a simple, yet incredibly powerful, three-letter word, and it has changed my life. For as long as I can remember, I've said yes to opportunities and experienced something amazing. I understand that for many women, saying YES to the unknown can be incredibly intimidating and outright paralyzing. For me, if I don't say YES, I can't help but wonder what would have happened.

How about you? How would you ever know if making the courageous decision would have an undeniable, positive impact on your life and the lives of those you love? I guess for me the "what if's" have always been way more terrifying than saying YES to the unknown.

I've come to understand, though, that we aren't guaranteed success every single time we say YES and accept a new opportunity. We may instead have a new experience which will teach us a valuable lesson. So, the more I say YES, the more opportunities appear along my journey. Chances are, the people you admire and look up to today are where they are because they had the courage to say YES, felt the fear, but went ahead with their decision anyway. Always remember this quote from Wayne Gretzky: "You miss 100 percent of the shots you don't take."

YES, I WILL BE YOUR WIFE!

I was 19 years old and working as a bank teller in a suburb outside of Chicago. It was early Friday evening after a very busy day at the bank. In those days, direct deposit didn't exist, and everyone came to the bank to deposit or cash their paychecks. There was a young man, Luis, who was a regular customer at the bank. He would come in every couple of weeks on payday, and I had seen him before and thought he was handsome. I never said anything to him or to anyone, but this Friday he walked in, walked up to my window to cash his check, and then asked me out. I was nervous but said YES, and we went to the movies that evening, dancing the next, and to church and lunch on Sunday. It was the perfect weekend and the start of a relationship with the most wonderful man who would later become my husband.

Luis and I dated for five years before he asked me to be his wife. Saying YES to Luis' marriage proposal was an incredible experience and definitely a YES that has changed my life forever. I recently read that besides knowing God as our savior, choosing our spouse is the most important decision we will ever make. Now, after almost 16 years of marriage, I understand why this statement is true. My personal growth and my ability to say YES more often has been in large part due to the support and love I've received from my husband since day one. He is my best friend, the person who never doubts my ability to do great things, an outstanding father, and someone who I respect and love more every day. Thank you, Mr. Regalado for being my rock when I've needed you most, my best friend, for believing in me always, and for constantly encouraging me to become the best possible version of myself.

YES, I WILL DO IT SCARED!

The second YES that changed my life happened when I was 22 years old. I had just finished college and was beginning what I thought would be my professional career. I originally went to school and became a radiologic technologist, specializing in the field of radiation therapy. As a radiation therapist, I was making a bit under six figures a year and thought this was what I wanted to do for the rest of my life, but I was wrong. A few months after I finished college and started working as a radiation therapist, I was invited to attend an event where a friend would share a business opportunity with a multi-level marketing company that I would accept that very same day.

I was very familiar with the products presented at the event. My mom, my sister, and I had used the products for years, but I had never known about the business opportunity behind them. The presentation began and I was captivated. Until then, I had never considered owning my own business. Nevertheless, I said YES to the opportunity right away, purchased my starter kit, and invested in some inventory. Then, my thoughts began to paralyze me. I started thinking of all the reasons why this was a bad idea and the reasons I would fail, when moments earlier, I had been so eager to embrace all the possibilities. I'm not sure why, but as human beings, we tend to focus more on the reasons we can't achieve a goal instead of the reasons we can.

I quickly acknowledged what I was feeling and immediately told myself that I wouldn't quit before I even started. I decided I would listen to my gut, because it was my first impression and I still felt it was worth pursuing. I decided I would do it, even though I was scared. I knew I would be more afraid of what would happen if I didn't try, than what would happen if I did. I immediately got into my car, drove away, and started on what would be a 17-year journey as part of one of the largest network marketing companies in the world. I achieved many goals along my journey, met some incredible leaders and friends, and gained confidence, knowledge, and wisdom along the way.

WHAT IF I HAD SAID NO?

I often think about the day I said YES to that business opportunity. What if I had allowed fear to convince me I wasn't good enough? What if I had believed that because I was incredibly shy and extremely introverted there was no way I would be able to share my products with others and find success as a business owner? What if I had entertained all the doubts, accepted that the decision was a mistake and told my friend to cancel everything? To encourage you to say YES to the next great opportunity you are given, let me share some of the most important experiences that saying YES has given me.

Shortly after Luis and I were married, I became pregnant with my son Luis Abraham who is now 13 years old. Less than two months after he was born, I found out I was expecting my second bundle of joy, my daughter, Lujan Anahi, who is now 12 years old and my only girl. We thought our family was complete when we found out we were expecting a third miracle. Juan Manuel, who is now nine years old, arrived to complete our family. Being an entrepreneur and able to work from home gave me the opportunity to raise my children and to be an active participant in their lives instead of a spectator. I believe children are a gift, and it is critical that we don't allow distractions and other less important things pull us away from the precious responsibility. Our babies don't come with a manual, but they surely need our love and attention.

The next experience happened on October 12, 2016, when my mother was diagnosed with one of the most aggressive forms of brain cancer called Glioblastoma Multiforme (GBM). GBMs are malignant and fast growing. When my sisters and I were told that there wasn't much we could do for her, there was no way we would believe it. Our mother was our rock, the strongest and most courageous woman I knew. We immediately began to do research and look for alternative medical care that would offer her the opportunity to fight for her life. We did all we could but unfortunately, our mother passed away eight months later.

The reason I am sharing this experience is because I am forever grateful for being able to care for my mom during the last eight months of her life. I could have never known that the YES to a business opportunity from more than 14 years earlier would have allowed me to step away from my business for those eight months without anyone asking why or how long I would be gone, worrying about using my vacation or personal days, or losing a job because they couldn't hold my position for that length of time. The courage to say YES gave me the opportunity to give my mom a priceless gift... my time.

YES, I WILL START WITHOUT KNOWING HOW!

I am addicted to learning and growing. My growth tool of choice is either audiobooks or podcasts, and as a result, I am constantly adding a new audiobook to my Audible account and pressing play to yet another episode from one of my favorite podcasts. As I was listening to a podcast episode about a year ago, something someone said inspired me and planted a seed to start my own podcast. I'm not going to lie; fear started to creep in, and I again started to come up with all the reasons why I couldn't do it. It took a few months, but I did the research and soon I was the host of the *Perfectly Imperfect with Leslie Regalado Podcast!*

It was surreal to see my face next to so many of my favorite podcasters on the different podcast platforms, and as I began to share episodes, I grew more and more excited. Before I knew it, I was recording an episode with Jackie Camacho-Ruiz who is the creator of the Today's Inspired Latina book series. During our conversation, my admiration for this courageous, brilliant, and innovative Latina leader grew with every word she spoke. Soon, we finished recording and what followed would change my life. Jackie asked me to be a part of the Today's Inspired Latina family. I agreed, and here we are. You are reading my story, and I am now a published author because I had the courage to say YES again. I am beyond grateful and want to thank Jackie for allowing her light to shine, for never playing small, and understanding that as she grows into the best version of herself, she's giving so many others permission to do the same.

Saying YES to an opportunity and staying the course to discover where it leads is one of the most liberating and empowering gifts you can give yourself. When you take a leap of faith, doubts disappear. So, say YES often, because the truth is, no matter where we end up and who ends up there with us, it's exactly the way it's supposed to be. Our mistakes make us who we are. We learn and we grow with every choice we make. I'll leave you with this quote from A.R. Lucas: "If there's even a slight chance of getting something that will make you happy, risk it. Life's too short, and happiness is too rare."

REFLECTION QUESTIONS

1. Think back to a time when you had the courage to say yes to an opportunity. Did it lead you to achieving a goal or did it teach you a valuable lesson?

2. What would happen if you stopped allowing fear of the unknown to dictate your decision-making, and instead started listening to your gut and saying YES to more amazing opportunities?

3. Now, it's time to take action and exercise your courage muscle. In the next 24-48 hours, take a chance and say YES to an opportunity. Then, email me and share your experience. I cannot wait to read your email.

BIOGRAPHY

Leslie Regalado is the daughter of Mexican immigrants. She lived in Anaheim, California, until her father, Juan Manuel Quiñones, passed away. She relocated to Chicago with her mother and two younger sisters. Leslie was the first college graduate in her family, earning a B.S. in Radiologic Sciences from Southern Illinois University. Two years later, she left her radiology career to pursue an opportunity with one of the world's largest network marketing companies. Over the next 17 years, she reached the top two percent of the sales force, and earned many impressive prizes.

Leslie started the *Perfectly Imperfect with Leslie Regalado* podcast in September of 2019, where she shares tangible advice and valuable conversations with some perfectly imperfect human beings in hopes of inspiring others to pursue their dreams.

Leslie is the founder and CEO of W.E. Lead Society, an online networking community which helps women discover exciting possibilities and opportunities to expand their network with like-minded women. They offer life and business tips, and educational courses to help women become their best selves.

Leslie lives near Chicago, Illinois, with her husband, Luis Regalado, and their three children, Luis Abraham, Lujan Anahi, and Juan Manuel.

Leslie Regalado
leslieq26@gmail.com
www.facebook.com/leslie.regalado

Alexandria Rios Taylor & Andrea Rios McMillian

"It's your responsibility to cultivate your development."

Our life has been blessed two-fold. Since we were born, we've been sharing a double measure of joy, pain, love, and success. As twins, duality is our birthright. It is a constant reminder that we are complementary, interconnected, and interdependent. The Eastern philosophy of yin and yang manifests and demonstrates the phenomena of harmony and balance through contrary forces, both success and failure, victory and defeat.

SISTERHOOD

We are sisters of the soul, truly half of the other. We were birthed into an inheritance filled with instant companionship, connection, and shared identity. Growing up, our battle for identity was like many other second and third generation LatinX youth. We sought to find our place, and figure out how our home-world and our school-world could merge and find harmony. We lived in a predominantly low-income, Hispanic community. Our family got by on food stamps and *segunda*, or second-hand, clothes. We were raised by a single mother who did her best to make ends meet. We lived humbly and relied heavily on church donations and food pantry visits to support our daily needs. However, thanks to our mother's insistence on getting a good education, we valued learning and knew that education was our ticket to a better life.

Educated in the town next door, an all-white, affluent community with a very low Latino population, we struggled to fit in and were very confused about social constructs and identity. We were encouraged to take ESL (English as a second language) classes even though we spoke perfect English, and listened to Selena before Madonna.

Our mother had a different last name than ours. We were used to cousins, aunts, and grandparents living with us for extended periods of time while most of our classmates made fun of our multi-generational or collective living environments. Setting us even further apart, we wore fishtail bangs, hoop earrings, and black-lined lipstick, whereas our school friends wore Abercrombie & Fitch with Birkenstock sandals. The everyday subtleties and stark contrasts of social life between a rich suburban school and a poor Latino neighborhood confused us and made us feel like we had to "pick" sides or, worse, reject the others' existence.

We fought hard to earn good grades while friends at home would call us *güeras* and say that we "talked white," when in reality, at school, we were poor Hispanic girls who were destined to slip through the cracks. We recognized our disadvantages and knew that we had something to prove. It took us both years of growth and reflection to fully become comfortable with our two environments and appreciate the balance that would eventually allow each world to coexist peacefully. It was a challenge, but we learned how to embrace the sum of both of our identities, and became open to beautiful friendships and wonderful mentors.

As sisters, we became really close in college, lived in dorms right next to each other, and found ourselves in the same social circles. We were both ambitious and eager to do well for our families and our communities.

As adults, we called each other on the phone numerous times a day, every day. We told each other everything, and left very little unturned. In our 20's, we shared clothes, shoes, exchanged cooking recipes, and swapped makeup tips. As we aged into our middle 30's, we began to focus more on health, wellness, and mental fortitude. We challenged each other to think critically, and brainstormed solutions to inequalities around us. It was during that time we fell in love with running, discovered a passion for fitness and strength training, and realized that there is power through discipline. We also learned to leverage time to our advantage.

Our first real fight didn't occur until we were 35 years old. We had heard of family feuds but never understood how families ever became fragile or divided. It wasn't until we had our first heart-to-heart disagreement that our obstinate personalities defied our empathy and our willful objections turned divisive. It was truly a time of learning, growing, and forgiving. We realized that no matter how close we were, or how like-minded we were raised, our distinct personalities allowed us to own unique perspectives that aren't always shared or valued.

The real test to our maturity was reflective in how we chose to forgive, move past the pain, and step into reconciliation with love and acceptance. To anyone struggling with being separated from a family member over pride, anger, or resentment; let it go. It isn't worth it.

MOTHERHOOD

Together, we have cried tears of joy as we've watched our kids take their first steps, perform in their first recitals, and drive their first car. Motherhood is an adventure that we were both blessed to have although our journeys were starkly different.

For Andrea, teenage motherhood was a reality. At 19 and a freshman in college, Andrea found herself pregnant, unwed, and questioning how she was going to finish college with a baby in tow. Trying to raise a baby is difficult for any mother, let alone for someone so young. It was not unusual for her to take her son with her to college classes, or sacrifice college events and social gatherings, in order to pick up extra work shifts to make ends meet. There were many days where the burden of young motherhood seemed heavy and isolating.

Alex, after witnessing the strain that parenting young could cause, dove into academia, and delayed marriage and kids. Her grandmother 's questions were endless, *¿cuándo te vas a casar? y ¿cuándo vas a tener hijos?* (When are you getting married? And when are you going to have children?) By the time she was 30, and was ready to start a family, no one had prepared her for the trials that awaited her as she began to "age out" of her biological clock. The heartache of infertility set in and applied pressure to her faith, her body, and the fertility specialists who helped her conceive after five miscarriages.

Eventually, we both found immense pain and joy in our destined pathways. We were made whole by the most miraculous human beings that God could have ever chosen for us, and if given the option, we would both choose our distinct journeys all over again! We both learned how to lean on each other through those highs and lows, witnessed how perfect yin and yang really is, and how life is a full rotation of balanced energy, between the good and the bad, the darkness and the sun. The healing and joy that was birthed from pain and heartache will always be our story to share and tell.

EVERYTHING IN BETWEEN

So where are we now? What did we learn? Was there ever really a *right way*? Regardless of the challenges, we were able to transcend our situations. We became fiercely protective of each other, and compassion filled our hearts. We learned that no road is perfect. We embraced each other, and finally understood that pathways are different roads that lead us through the same shared human experiences.

Andrea graduated college with her son and husband in the front row, and became a local leader, bringing technological innovation to her hometown of Aurora, Illinois. She has an entrepreneurial mindset, and is always vested in promoting girls in the technology and business sectors. She created a podcast, *Tuesdays with Andrea*, that discusses life's big questions, relevant hot topics, and personal journeys. *Tuesdays with Andrea* features real, everyday nightlights around people of all ages, cultures, and backgrounds. It's a place for fresh perspective, authentic connection, useful information, and personal wisdom.

Alex became a high school assistant principal and devotes her life to inspiring and motivating youth through teaching and publishing. She has climbed the academic ranks to empower underrepresented youth by reminding them to dream big and be fearless. She partnered with Jackie on bringing the *Today's Inspired Young Latina: Dreams and Aspirations from the Next Generation* book series to life. Volume I and II were such successes that they are currently working on Volume III!

As you navigate your way, our advice is simple. Let's stop questioning why our path is *our* path. Let's give ourselves permission to grow into our true power and mature into the space where we truly belong. Let's rest in the truth that our voice is worthy of the story that only we can write. Set your own rules, champion the *little* victories, and learn to nurture your relationships along the way. The right people will show up for you in times of need and demonstrate that *people* are the illuminators of our pathways. And once you make it, know that it becomes your responsibility to then show up for others because the world needs more compassion and empathy.

The ancient teachings of duality, yin and yang, reveals harmony and abundance. That if one door closes, another always opens. That if disappointment comes, we can make a decision to learn from it and move forward. That if something doesn't serve us anymore, we can change the narrative and "close that chapter." So if you are in the midst of fog and confused about your pathway, use these guiding questions to make your future clear.....

- Who *am* I? What *are* my values?
- What do I want? And *why*?
- How do I want to *show up for others*?
- Have I ever really *challenged* my beliefs?
- *Who* do I need around me?
- What *resources* can I leverage?

Be the person you're meant to be, and don't let your past get in the way. It's your responsibility to cultivate your development. It's not your fault for how you were raised, but it is your responsibility to heal. Only you can decide how you choose to perceive the world. Focus on your power and purpose, and know that it's worth it to show up to your future!

REFLECTION QUESTIONS

1. What have you learned from the path you have taken in life?

2. How is "duality" represented in your life?

3. How have you healed from the traumas of your past and leveraged them for your future?

ANDREA RIOS MCMILLIAN & ALEXANDRA RIOS TAYLOR

Andrea Rios McMillian develops new business strategies and partner relations for CompTIA's Creating IT Future workforce programs nationwide. She was responsible for expanding workforce development initiatives in Chicago and spearheading partnership growth for Chicago's Early College STEM Schools. Andrea joined Creating IT Futures with 10 years of business development and management experience, and is based at their headquarters in Downers Grove, Illinois. Her passion drives her to serve on the Aurora Hispanic Heritage Advisory Board, which organizes fundraising and scholarship awards for local students.

Alexandria Rios Taylor is a high school Assistant Principal in the southwest suburbs of Chicago. She recently partnered with Jackie Camacho-Ruiz on the anthology entitled *Today's Inspired Young Latina: Dreams and Aspirations from the Next Generation* series. Alex is currently pursuing her doctorate degree in educational administration at Aurora University as she examines the pipeline of diverse educators. She holds a master's degree in leadership and administration from Benedictine University and completed her undergraduate studies at North Central College. Alex was later recognized by her alma mater and received the Sesquicentennial Award in education as a top educator in her decade.

Andrea Rios McMillian
tuesdayswithandrea@gmail.com

Alexandria Rios Taylor
alexandria.rios@gmail.com

Vany Hernández

"True fulfillment and true success in life comes from fully living out your God-given purpose and calling."

I grew up in a small town called Benque Viejo Del Carmen in the country of Belize. I recall fond memories growing up, being crowned queen of my town, selling little bags of popcorn at school, winning various spelling bee competitions, dancing at cultural nights, and always making the high honor roll list. I remember saying that one of my dreams was to visit the United States. I was definitely an outgoing little girl with big dreams.

My parents are divorced, and I am the oldest of two. I was not fortunate to have both my parents together as I was growing up, so I was forced to become strong and independent at a very young age. My mom had to travel every day for her domestic work to ensure we had all that we needed. Unfortunately, my dad was never really there for us, but despite his mistakes, I love him, and I've forgiven him. Every experience I had with my parents molded me into the person I am today. Some were happy experiences, most were very sad, and I would need more than a chapter to write about them. But I focused on what I could learn from each one to become a better version of myself and move forward in my life.

MY SEARCH FOR PURPOSE AND FULFILLMENT

I remember saying goodbye to my mom and my little brother in June 2004. I was about to fulfill one of my dreams, which was coming to the United States. I was so excited, but at the same time, I was sad to leave my family and close friends. I had so many hopes when I arrived, however I was faced with the reality that my job opportunities were limited as an immigrant.

I started working as a nanny. I got up early every day to take the train to get to work. I did that for 10 years and I was not really enjoying it, but it provided me a weekly paycheck and allowed me to live a good lifestyle, which at that time was enough for me, or so I thought. I was just on survival mode like most of the people out there, going to work every day, then coming home, watching TV, sleeping, and doing the same thing over and over again. But one day in October 2008, I got a call from my mom's boss in Belize. She gave me the tragic news that my little brother had passed away. I remember crying on the floor; it seemed like a nightmare. Unfortunately, due to my status, I couldn't be there. It was one of the saddest days in my life, but also a turning point for me.

As I reflected on the life I was living, I noticed a great feeling of unfulfillment within me. Even though I had a good husband and a good paying job that allowed me to live well, deep down I felt something was missing. I knew deep down that there was more for me. I thought about the hopes and the dreams I had before coming to this country. Leaving my family back home and now losing my one and only brother had to be worth it, and so my search for purpose and fulfillment began. I tried to do different things, and one of them was network marketing. I was hooked on the trainings they gave to the business owners and that's where my personal growth and transformation began.

After five years of it, I decided to leave network marketing behind. Even though I was growing, I wasn't really enjoying it, and it felt more like a job than a business. I was still looking for fulfillment, and I remember asking God to show me my purpose and to place the right people in my life to help me go where He wanted to take me. I prayed, I read books, I attended events, I learned from motivational speakers online, I looked at YouTube videos, and that's how I came to know about life coaching and online business. I was so excited to learn more about it that I didn't hesitate to get my first coaching certification. I decided to start an online business, and for a while, I just concentrated on how I could successfully launch it.

Even though I had great mentors and coaches to help me out, I just couldn't seem to get up and running. I had so many limiting beliefs and mindset blocks that paralyzed me and shook my confidence. For years, I sabotaged myself. I struggled a lot, even though I had the tools to help me with those limiting beliefs. However, I serve a great God, and He started placing the right people in my path to help me see where those beliefs and mindset blocks were coming from. I still had so much to heal, and He continued working in me.

Gradually, I started to gain clarity around my purpose. I felt called to help women experience the same transformation that I did. It was still a bit unclear, but at least I had an idea of where to start.

FACING MY FEARS

I tried my best to start showing up in the online space by sharing posts and writing some blog posts, but one thing I could not do was show myself in video or go live. I was so scared of being on camera. I started to think about when I was a little girl. What had happened to that outgoing girl who could stand in front of hundreds of people for spelling bee contests and cultural nights? I realized that I still had so many fears and insecurities in me, but I continued facing them. I would try to start up my business, and then I would stop. It was like a pattern I had, but one day I had a serious conversation with myself. I decided that it was time for me to stop playing small and start showing up, even if things weren't so clear and perfect.

I continued having my doubts, thinking that maybe my business desire was not from God, or that I am not qualified enough, but I couldn't imagine not doing it. I was starting to feel so fulfilled and felt so aligned to it. That was when I started feeling I was living my purpose. And so today I am building that business, helping women step confidently into who God created them to be. On those days when I feel disappointed or when things are not happening as I would like, this is what keeps me moving forward.

For me, what I do is more than just a business; it's a calling. And it is not only about the money, but the impact I can make in women's lives. It's about the legacy I will leave the day God calls me to heaven. It's about contributing to the Kingdom and being able to contribute to great causes and make this world a better place.

If you have a desire to share a message or make an impact in some way, start with what you have. Yes, you will have fears. Yes, you will have doubts, but you are more than a conqueror. God has equipped you with everything necessary to become who you were created to be. You can do this, sister!

I might not know where you come from or the things you have endured in life, but one thing I know is that you were created for more. You were not created to feel stuck forever and live an unfulfilled life. God created you to thrive and prosper and make an impact in this world. Your gifts and talents are needed to serve a certain group of people out there. Your message needs to be heard. Identify your passions, find what lights you up and start with what you have. When you start showing up, God begins to bring people to you, and he starts opening doors. I know it because he's been doing it with me. When I decided to start walking in faith and action, he started bringing the women to me who needed to hear my message. I've received messages from women telling me how they've benefited from what I've shared through my content, services, and in-person events.

Today I am writing this because I decided to show up and believe that I was created for more. I remember attending a *Today's Inspired Latina* event a few years ago. I went to support one of my dear friends who was also a co-author. I was so inspired by all the women and their speeches. I recall thinking that one day I wanted to be part of *Today's Inspired Latina* and I envisioned myself participating. I even posted it on my vision board. And today I am here, writing part of my story for Volume VIII. I still can't believe this is happening, but it certainly is.

YOUR TURN

I hope that part of my story inspired you to step powerfully into the purposeful woman God created you to be. True fulfillment and true success in life comes from fully living out your God-given purpose and calling. Maybe for you that calling could be a business, a non-profit organization, a ministry, or another God-sized dream. Whatever it is, I know it's in your heart because God has placed it there, and He has given you everything to fulfill it. Don't underestimate your gifts, talents, passions, abilities, knowledge, and everything you've been through. They are there for you to serve and help others. True success in life is not measured by how much you have, but by how much of a difference you make with what you have.

Surround yourself with people who encourage you and lift you up. Nowadays, there are so many ways to connect with people who are there to support you. I couldn't be doing what I am doing now if it wasn't for the great mentors and coaches that I've had. I have learned from each one of them and I continue learning every day. There will always be something new to learn and help us grow. During your journey, you will face ups and downs, but never forget that you are here for a purpose and that purpose will be the driving force for you to keep going when things are not going the way you'd like. Don't be afraid to fail, for that only makes you wiser and stronger. Have faith and trust in God that everything will come in its perfect time.

Believe that you were made for more!

REFLECTION QUESTIONS

1. Are you truly living a fulfilled and purposeful life?

2. How are you making a difference in other people's lives?

3. What does true success mean to you?

BIOGRAPHY

Vany Hernández is a bilingual Latina living in Chicago. She is passionate about inspiring and helping women step confidently into the purposeful women God created them to be. She firmly believes that when a woman walks in her God-given purpose and what she is called to do, she is able to feel truly fulfilled.

Vany was born and grew up in a small town called Benque Viejo del Carmen in the beautiful country of Belize. In 2004, she moved to Chicago where she now lives with her husband Marlon and her two kids, Kelvin and Iker.

Vany has an associate's degree in international business, is a certified life coach, and is also a style coach. Vany loves learning and investing in her personal, spiritual, and professional development.

On most days, you can see her working on her laptop and spending time with her family. She is a lover of all things Parisian and of personal style. She enjoys reading, spending time with God, and having coffee with her friends.

One of Vany's fun dreams is to visit Paris and have a photoshoot in front of the Eiffel Tower. She definitely looks forward to that day.

Vany Hernández
www.vanyhernandez.com
773-799-5067

Damaris Samolinski

"We need to tell those we love how significant they are in our lives."

I have known many people that do not have a relationship with their mothers. This has troubled me for a very long time. Although I know there are different circumstances that would prevent people from having a healthy and meaningful relationship with their mothers, it is disturbing to know that some people never reconcile with their mothers. You see, I grew up without a mother, and I would give anything in the world to be able to see mine in a physical body so that I could touch her, embrace her, and see her bright smile.

For me, that's impossible in this lifetime, because once the soul leaves its physical body, it takes another form. If you believe in reincarnation as I do, we believe that the soul has no end and no beginning. A body only comes around once and will never return. If a soul decides to reincarnate, it takes on another body. We should cherish the time we now have and make the best of it because we will never see our body again. It continuously takes on different bodies, in different lifetimes, for the purpose of evolution—or in other words, for the purpose of raising its consciousness.

DEPARTURES

Many people say that they love someone but fail to express it to them. We need to tell those we love how significant they are in our lives. Otherwise, they can cross over into the next life with the presumption that they were never loved and we will be left behind with feelings of regret because we never conveyed our love to them.

I was not even nine years old on that fateful Friday when my mother left our house to help her good friend Sylvia move her daughter into an apartment. Sylvia's daughter was pregnant and making the move to escape her baby's father. That evening, my mother did not return home. On Monday, my mother, her friend and the daughter were found knifed to death in Sylvia's daughter's apartment. Unfortunately, the case remains unsolved. We never found out who did it, even though the police questioned many suspects, including the daughter's boyfriend and my father, who had finalized a very contentious divorce from my mother just two months earlier. Even though the case ran cold, for years, influenced by my mother's family, I struggled with the possibility that my father could have killed my mother.

Back then, how could I have ever known that my contact with my mother in this life would only be for a few short years? In my mind, I thought I had all the time in the world to convey my love for her. I grew up feeling guilty for not letting her know how deeply I loved and needed her; I never really had the chance to share my feelings. Sometimes, we don't realize just how much people need to hear the words, "I love you." It could make all the difference in the world.

REVELATIONS

On a whim one day, I decided to try a meditation exercise. I wanted to perform a regression on myself, which is a way of reviewing a past life event in a different way. It is like viewing a movie and learning to see something from another's perspective. I wanted to revisit my mother's relationship with my father and how unfairly she was treated.

My mother had already been through one bad marriage, then found my father and gave birth to me. Long before she was killed, her spirit was gone. She endured my father's alcoholism, as well as the hurtful behavior of my brothers, who did not choose their girlfriends well. I think after a while, she just lost the will to fight. Pain and suffering ravaged her body, mind, and soul.

As I entered the exercise, I saw that there was so much that I failed to notice as I lived through the chaos of my family life. I was able to become me, but outside of my body, to experience things not as an eight-year-old girl, but as I am today. It was as if I was watching the movie of my life in my mind's eye and looking from the outside in. I was able to see things that I could not see before because I was too young, emotionally involved, and simply unaware of any problem. In other words, I was me but with emotions on a higher plane.

One of the biggest issues we as humans have is that we are emotional beings, and when we allow our emotions to take control of us, we can't see clearly. Therefore, our feelings often obscure the solutions to our problems. We have different levels of consciousness, and emotions that are felt from the lower levels of consciousness can become clouded. They create separation and above all, they create blame and judgment. In my meditation exercise, I was viewing the experiences of my life from my heart center which is a higher level of consciousness. From this level, which is as highly elevated as the soul, all I had was compassion for all involved, including me.

I gained transformative insight through this regression exercise. It not only gave me a better understanding of my mother's life, but it allowed me to understand the meaning of my life, too. As a result, I was able to comprehend why her death occurred, the wisdom that came from being her daughter, and the lessons that I had to learn from my experience. I concluded that I needed to feel the lack of everything I wanted in order to understand its significance. Perhaps I would never have known how to love so deeply, become independent, and gain an incredible trust in God if she was alive. In life, I believe you have to experience the lack of something in order to gain appreciation for it when you have it.

For example, I grew up without a mother and I had to learn how to mother myself. After losing her, I couldn't really rely on anyone, so I learned to rely on myself. I began working at the age of 15 years old, just as my mother did. All the qualities my mother possessed, I gained as an adult.

My father played an extraordinary role in her life, and every event after they met had a domino effect that spiraled downward until her death. However, unbeknownst to all of us at the time, everything was in divine and perfect order. My father only set the wheel in motion for what was to come. In my regression exercise, I was able to tap into her being in order to see, feel, smell, and sense everything as if I was her.

I see so clearly the story of our lives now, and I can understand everyone's role. I am able to forgive everything that I felt was wrong in my life because I know there was purpose and meaning within every event and circumstance that I experienced. Forgiveness is the key to opening the door of my self-imposed prison. As a result of this exercise, I have awakened to true and unconditional love for my mother and father, and for the roles they both played in my life. Without those tragic experiences, I would never have sought the light that led me to my spiritual awakening!

A SIGN

My father had been sick for many years with diabetes. He suffered long with this debilitating illness and on his birthday, April 4, 2013, I went to visit him in the hospital. When I entered his room, he told me that his entire body was aching. He said that he was ready to go "home" to God. So, I decided to give him a little Reiki. Reiki is a universal life-force energy that comes through the practitioner onto the recipient which brings comfort to anyone that needs it. I wanted to help him and ease some of the pain he was feeling. As I ran my hands over his body, I asked my mother to help him through this process. Even though he was not a kind husband to her, and caused her much grief, I asked her to forgive him, and for her omnipresence to wait for him on the other side to help ease his transition and bring him comfort.

Twelve days later, on April 16, my mother's birthday, I woke up to a phone call at 8:32 a.m. My father had peacefully passed away in his sleep. To me, this was a great confirmation that my mother had heard and answered my prayers, and helped greet him on the other side. I believed they were both in peace with each other, with no more turmoil between them.

Life is not about possessions, status, or trophies; life is about love and relationships. Let your loved ones know that you love them while you still have a chance. If your mother is still here, reach out and tell her you love her no matter what the circumstances, because chances are, there's more than meets the eye. There is probably a bigger picture that you cannot see from a limited perspective, or from the lower emotions of the ego. Remember, the door to your freedom will open when you finally forgive those you thought had wronged you. Take advice from Satish Kumar: *"I forgive all beings, I ask for forgiveness from all beings, I make friends with all beings, I have no enemies."*

REFLECTION QUESTIONS

1. How has your mother influenced your life for the better and the worse?

2. What do you believe about the soul, and how does that affect the way you live your life?

3. Who do you need to forgive in your life? How will you do it?

BIOGRAPHY

Damaris Samolinski is an Interfaith Minister and Reverend and has had her own spiritual practice in Long Island, New York, since 2011. She is a spiritual life coach, and teaches many workshops on metaphysical topics which assist in raising the human consciousness.

She believes that raising one's consciousness can eradicate human suffering on all levels. She is very passionate about her area of expertise, which also includes energy work, aromatherapy, gemstones, the chakras, and teachings about the four levels of the human body which include the spiritual, mental, emotional, and physical layers, and how they interconnect with one another. After discovering that this knowledge is imperative for every individual's well-being, she needed to share it with everyone interested in learning about its importance.

Before devoting her life to her work, she suffered the tragic loss of her mother at a very young age. This traumatic event initiated an endless search for the meaning of life and death, and how to overcome grief in order to continue living on purpose. Through this life-long search for answers, she discovered that within her trauma there were gifts of enlightenment, spiritual guidance, illumination, soul liberation, and personal blessings.

Damaris Samolinski
damaris.samolinski@gmail.com
(631)335-8892

Abigail Silva Michel

"Any time in your life you can reinvent yourself and choose who you want to become."

I was born in Mexico City in 1972 to my mother Irma and my father Luis. My parents told me how they longed for a daughter, so I was received with a lot of love. I grew up feeling very desired by my parents.

I was raised in a family of five, with my parents, my sister, and one brother. I am the oldest. I recall that our childhoods were quite beautiful, and we were raised by loving parents, who always strived to give us the best. They educated us with Catholic faith, showed us respect, and made each of us feel unique and special. They always told us that they had no favorites. My parents loved me for being the oldest, my brother for being the middle child as well as the only boy, and my little sister for being the youngest in our family.

I attended the Universidad de las Americas in Mexico City in the 1990s, and earned my license in human communications and studied speech/language pathology and audiology. I completed my education in four years, and learned to work with children with hearing, language, and learning difficulties. After that, I earned my specialization in special education and early intervention, as I finally completed my master's degree in linguistic disabilities. All my life I have had teachers who lived with little means, but taught me so much. I've also had other excellent changes that marked my life forever. Their wisdom remains in my memory, and I apply what they once shared with me as teachers to my current work. Surely, I believe they would be proud of me, to see how well they taught me.

A NEW COUNTRY, A NEW PURPOSE

Immigrating to the United States was unexpected. My husband was recruited for a new job opportunity, so we had to start a new life in a different country, far from our family and far from home. At the time, I was worried about facing new challenges, language barriers, and adapting to a different culture. Although it was very difficult to face so many different changes, in the end I believe it was a good decision to embrace this opportunity, create a better life for my children, and advance my life purpose to help others.

Coming to the United States gave me the opportunity to start working with a community that soon stole my heart. Currently, I work in a school where 90 percent of the population is Hispanic. Working here has brought me so much joy and has taught me a lot. And so, I wanted to do something for this community to show my gratitude.

In this work, I really found my life purpose: giving back to the community and being able to change or impact the life of a student forever. My work allows me to spend many hours with my students and to get to know them on a personal level. They generally have a lot of confidence as they share their stories with me. I have heard stories of all kinds of sexual, physical, and emotional abuse, or other forms of neglect that I never imagined could happen to such young students.

My position gives me the opportunity to talk with the students one-on-one since they are arranged in smaller group sessions. We work on individualized instruction in mathematics and language arts. However, I realized that there was something else, something more important than school issues, in the lives of these students. There were issues relating to their family and home life.

One day, I decided that I could no longer hear their stories and do nothing. I listened to their sorrows and concerns of their personal lives and began to hear stories that were so heartbreaking I could not believe it. For many students, school became their "safe place" which seems to be the case for many Hispanic children in this country.

AN IDEA IS BORN

I know through the stories of victims that physical and emotional abuse can change a life forever. However, I also believe that at any time in your life you can reinvent yourself and choose who you want to become. I will never forget the time a kindergartener told me that the son of her friend's mother sexually abused her and her little brother. The boy was in high school and in the evenings, he sexually abused his own younger brother and my student while making them watch porn movies in the afternoon. This was a very difficult story to hear, and I immediately reported it to the police.

Another story that impacted me was from a student who told me how her father physically and emotionally abused her mother, and also gave out verbal beatings and battering every day. One day he threw a pan of boiling water on her mother's chest in front of their children. In anguish and in fear of him, they all left the house that winter night and slept in the car. The next day, the girl arrived with the same clothes and without bathing, and she told me in tears what had happened. I had to call the police and DFSS (Department of Family and Support Services) and report the case. The dad went to prison and the kids were taken into custody by a family member as her mom recovered.

A final story that touched my heart was about a mother who beat her son horribly with different objects. One day my student came to school and showed me a mark he had gotten with a hot iron to his leg. I was in shock of how this heartless mother could abuse her own son in this inhumane way. I wondered again and again, how can you hurt your own son like that in such a violent way? How sad it is to know that there are so many women in the world who want to have a child to care for, love, and respect, but they are unable to have children. Yet, this lady was violently abusing her own son. Yet again, this was a case I had to report to DFSS.

As the students told me their stories of neglect, injustice, deportations, and deprivations, they felt relieved. They knew they could confide in me for my help and support and trust me to do the right thing to protect them from further harm. These students would always come back to me and say, "Thank you Maestra Silva, thank you for helping me, for listening to me, and accompanying me so I wouldn't feel so sad." I am the teacher who not only teaches them, but also understands and supports them. Above all, I am someone who cares deeply for their well-being on a heartfelt level.

I found a population of people who need me, and I needed, too. I have good relationships with the students, and they trust me a lot about their concerns or issues in life. I always listen to them, and they know they can count on me because besides being their teacher, I am someone they can confide in and help if they are in need. With this, I started to get more and more involved to see what else I could do to help them.

I realized that many parents and students felt better just by being heard and understood by someone else. Many said, "Thank you, Maestra Silva, for listening to me." The stories of my students inspired me to start the *"Conectando Corazones"* (Connecting Hearts) project. This project aims to help and accompany students and their families who need guidance in all aspects of life. I can identify and relate to them because I am also an immigrant. Being a minority and from another country can be very lonely. During difficult moments in life, it is good to have someone who understands you when you need guidance, or just simply to listen to you. Hearing my students' problems concerning their home lives made me think about the possibility of creating a space where students and parents could share a moment together to try to find a solution.

THE JOY OF CONNECTING

The idea of this project is also to bring in people who are specialized in different parenting issues to share their wisdom with the community. Raising children is not an easy task. Although there are many children whose parents cannot get involved in their academics, there are also many other parents with a great desire to learn about different parenting tactics. Then there are many parents who do want to help their children, but do not know how, and need an extra guide.

My project was born to help students in the early development stages to prevent problems in their future. We want healthy, happy children who live a life that is valued, and who want to grow into their adulthood with confidence and joy. But the only way it can be done is to give them a happy childhood. A happy child will become a happy adult. So investing time in children is investing time in our future.

Also, helping others gives you more than you imagine. The feeling is so beautiful that it becomes an addiction. In the end, not all the stories are sad. There are wonderful families who are very involved and supportive of their children. Students that I have had in the past are now are doing well and have graduated from high school or college.

To be a parent is to teach with love in the best way that you can. As a parent, there is no "operator's manual" for exactly how to educate our kids. We are allowed to make mistakes as we all are human, and find perfection within our imperfections. Within a group of fellow parents, we can share experiences and confide in one another about the journey of being a parent.

Do what moves you inside, what makes you vibrate. That is exactly how I feel when I help others through the *Conectando Corazones* project.

Seeing realities of others and listening to their stories makes you see the world from a different perspective. From another point of view, we are able to love and value more of what we already have. This community has provided me with so many beautiful moments, and I am thankful for every day that I can help my students in whatever ways that I can. The mothers and fathers as well as students have stolen my heart. They are an incredible community and group of people that motivate me every day to look for better things for my project and make it grow more and more each day. I love helping my community. I know that I can't change the world, but I can change my community. We can all contribute in a small way to improve our environment, and each other's lives.

REFLECTION QUESTIONS

1. How can you positively affect the lives of the children around you?

2. What do you do to help your community?

3. The last time you heard of any injustice taking place, how did you respond?

BIOGRAPHY

Abigail Silva is a beloved teacher and creator of *Conectando Corazones,* a project with a mission to empower young people and their families. Her father was a philanthropist and leader of a union in Mexico City. Doing so, he provided benefits for community, and lived a generous life for those who were less fortunate.

She follows in his footsteps by helping people in the community and generously giving her time and talent to those who are less fortunate. Learning from him, she wanted to continue the meaning of this legacy. And so, *Conectando Corazones* was born.

Abi has a lot of gratitude in her heart, and she believes she is very blessed with the life she has. She is grateful for her husband, children, mother, father, and siblings. By creating *Conectando Corazones*, she is able to give back to community, and especially the students.

Conectando Corazones fills her heart and the hearts of others by inspiring them to live life with happiness and purpose. Her mission is to empower the young and their families, as she hopes that they can work together to provide a bright future for the coming generations. Abigail hopes that one day her children will continue her work, and carry on the tradition. She believes it is very important to help the new generations as they are the future of our world.

Abigail Silva Michel
Suenoscorazones@gmail.com
224-805-0756

Monse Moreno

"We need connectedness and community to inspire us to become financially empowered."

Once you learn something, you can't unlearn it. In my case, when I learn something, I want to share it with everyone because at my core, my superpower is connecting. I am a connector of people, ideas, and information because I've experienced that knowledge and access to knowledge, is power. So, I want to share my personal money story so I can empower others.

THE FIRST STEP

I was 22 and had just graduated from Marquette University, and secured my first big job in Chicago. I had moved home after spending eight years away, first at a boarding school for senior high, and then college. Although I didn't know it, those eight years were the beginning of my money story. The eight years afterwards would build a future towards financial freedom.

The boarding school was Deerfield Academy in Massachusetts, and I was able to go because at the age of 14, I was courageous enough to seek out the Daniel Murphy Scholarship Fund (DMSF) and found a committee who believed in my potential. The DMSF gave me access to the highest quality secondary education, and exposure to a world of abundance and wealth that was very different from my Latino community on the south side of Chicago. It also created a bridge to college.

The DMSF also had created a caddie program that placed select scholars from Chicago in local college dorms in the north and western suburbs to work as caddies for the summer. We were then eligible to apply for the Chick Evans Scholarship, a 4-year scholarship for golf caddies. We worked Tuesday through Sunday, and counselors would drive us to the country club each day. It was hard work in Chicago's summer heat, but it was well worth it.

As young teenage girls, we spent the money exactly how you'd expect. We'd go to the mall or movies and eat out with our friends. It was summer, and we hadn't developed financially responsible behavior. And yet, I was committed and caddied for three full summers before applying for the scholarship in the fall of 2005.

My dedication and work ethic at the golf course, and at Deerfield, paid off when I was awarded the scholarship to attend Marquette University. I still had to cover some expenses over the four years, but I was the first in my family to attend college, and it was a crash course in making financial decisions on my own. I didn't learn these lessons or act without my parents and family; I always had their support. I just had to learn from afar.

As I look back, I learned an important money lesson through my teenage years. First, I was incredibly fortunate to have made the choices I did around scholarships and summer jobs, and those early decisions became a healthy foundation for adulthood.

THE SECOND STEP

I can't say I kicked off adulthood any differently than I did my teen years. I moved back home and kind of reverted back to those summer days of living with my friends. I wasn't familiar with the impact of investing early in 401Ks or brokerage accounts. Instead, I was doing things like going on road trips to Cedar Point with my coworkers and going to Paris with my boyfriend.

One day, when I was shopping in St. Charles, Illinois, I found a used book called *"The Smart Cookie's Guide to Making More Dough."* The cover featured five women and described how they created a money club to get smart and take control of their finances. I'd never even thought about money the way they did, and I was intrigued enough to buy the book.

It opened my eyes and put me on a path to financial literacy. *"The Smart Cookie's Guide"* made me realize "I didn't know what I didn't know" about money. While my family always supported and guided me to save and avoid debt, they hadn't taught me what was in the book. In fact, they had their own unanswered financial questions. From that moment on, I knew I was going to have to learn *for* them and not *from* them about money management.

The book was a hands on-guide that introduced me to new concepts, helped me question my habits, and inspired a curiosity to learn more. There is one exercise in the book which I thank for single-handedly putting me on a path to financial freedom. It was called "The Perfect Day." It asked me to put pen to paper and design my life. What would a perfect day for me be like? Where would I live? What would I do? What was I grateful for and how did I feel about my life? Up until that point, I had been living my life reactively, following a predetermined academic path and accepting what was put in front of me. But for the first time, I was spending time thinking. Really, really thinking about what I wanted, dreaming big and outside of what I could expect of someone in my situation.

The first time I did this exercise I was recently engaged. I wrote that I wanted to live in a little brick house with my husband. I would wake up and open the French doors in my bedroom to let the sun and warmth begin my day. I'd have breakfast and we'd head out to work. There I'd be challenged but satisfied in my work. I could take a break for yoga in the middle of the day, then go home after work, meet up with my best friend for tennis at dusk, and end my day with my hubby, watching a movie or planning our next vacation.

Dreaming about a perfect day was wonderful, but the difference was part two of the exercise. This part asked for the plan behind the perfect day. You would do your homework and create a plan. That was where the magic of intentionality came in. So, I researched home prices in neighborhoods I liked. I began learning about mortgages and interest. I also thought deeply about the kind of career I wanted that would make me feel grateful, excited, and accomplished, but also have the balance to have a quality life. I love to travel, so I had to make sure this life supported my lifestyle, financial, and personal goals. I started mapping the numbers and breaking them down by years and then months. At the end of the exercise I had a five-year plan to get to this perfect day. I share my perfect day with the hopes that you get creative and think outside of the box from what is expected, to what is extraordinary and possible for your life.

THE THIRD STEP

That single book was only the first of many ways I'd increase my financial literacy over the next eight years. I began reading and learning more, from paperbacks, to online blogs, money magazines, and podcasts. I followed personal finance personalities like Dave Ramsey and Suze Orman on Facebook and Instagram. I surrounded myself with opportunities to learn. The Smart Cookie authors were also career women themselves who, through their stories, inspired confidence in me to navigate my career. I was making career moves and seeing success, repeatedly. I'd accomplish one goal, and then launch another. I'd tackle new roles and negotiate bravely as I walked into the next. My husband and I were both slowly, but surely, along a healthy path to retirement when somewhere along the way, in the years after my first job, I was introduced to the FIRE movement.

FIRE stands for Financial Independence Retire Early, a community of people from all walks of life, investors who invest and save upwards of 50 percent or more of their income to hit an early retirement and actively participate in helping others do the same. The members of the community live virtually across social media groups and blogs where they freely share their journeys, their tips, tricks, and knowledge with one another.

I was immediately hooked by the idea and set my personal goal to "FIRE by 40." In joining these groups, I was surprised by the depth of my personal knowledge as I became more of a contributing member than a passive observer. But I also realized the knowledge being shared online within this self-selected community didn't include many people like me.

In the Latino community, money is often a taboo subject that isn't discussed and can at times result in feelings of shame or scarcity. The financial industry also has historically underserved Latinos; the systems and messages are not designed with us in mind. Even in 2020, while these institutions understand the market potential of Latinos, they still don't make it easy for them to participate or actively change negative feelings about the industry. Even then I could see that we need connectedness and community to inspire us to become financially responsible. I was connecting with the FIRE community, but not my Latino community.

That inspired me to share my money story and also spark conversations about personal finance more often. My new goal became to not only hit FIRE by 40, but to financially empower, connect, and inspire my family, my friends, my broad Latino community to achieve financial freedom. I began meeting with and supporting anyone who asked for help. My approach was to share positive stories and point people to the right resources for them to learn from our own community.

Eventually, I would have to scale these ideas in a different way to reach more people and make a real impact. One night at dinner, a friend inspired me to take a leap of faith on an idea I had considered for months. I did not have the confidence to bring my idea to life until she made me think of the people out there who needed to hear it from me. So, within a few weeks, I took the jump and created my own personal finance blog. It's www.HappyMoneyHappyLife.com, a personal-finance-meets-travel blog with the mission of inspiring Latinas and other ladies to cultivate a positive relationship with money, become financially empowered, and live their best life.

My money story shows how taking an active approach to learning about personal finance can help anyone reach even the most aggressive goals and, hopefully, one day achieve financial freedom. It is also full of many more ups and downs and lessons learned which I could add in greater detail, but then I'd be writing a novel. All I know is each time I share my money story, someone takes a piece of inspiration towards an action on their own journey, and that is what I hope for with all my heart.

REFLECTION QUESTIONS

1. What is your money story and what do you want it to be?

2. What would your "perfect day" look like?

3. How does your attitude towards money propel you or hold you back from creating the life you want?

BIOGRAPHY

Monse Moreno was born and raised on the south side of Chicago by two hard-working and loving parents, Maria and Daniel, alongside her brother, Ferran, and sister, Annabelle.

She attended Deerfield Academy through the Daniel Murphy Scholarship Fund. She went on to attend Marquette University as a Chick Evans Scholar. Being a golf caddie was her first job, but she went on to work in advertising sales at the Marquette Tribune which led her to a career in advertising and marketing.

Monse began at Starcom Mediavest Group and then moved to Pandora Media Inc. She married fellow DMSF and Chick Evans Scholar, Gus, and the two now live in Brookfield, Illinois. Passionate to support the Latino community both at home and at work, Monse is currently the global co-lead for Facebook's Latino employee resource group.

Monse Moreno
monse.m.moreno@gmail.com
@happymoneyhappylife

Jacqueline Bouvier

"Success is all-encompassing."

"I was born to be a leader!" This was my husband's reply when I asked him what I should share in this chapter. He said, "Just tell the *Latinitas* of this world that you were born to be a leader." As much as I wish that were true…it was not always the case.

NEW WAYS

My life has been a journey of self-discovery as a result of my tumultuous upbringing. However, I must attribute my success, strong character, and maturity to my childhood experiences. I grew up surrounded by the victim mentality and the impostor syndrome, due to a loss of my identity. You wouldn't think an identity is something a human being can easily lose. You are right, it's not! It isn't even easy to identify unless something more powerful than yourself, or certain shocking life events, shake you enough to open your eyes to the truth.

As an immigrant family, we migrated to the U.S., the land of opportunity, to achieve that so-called "American Dream" that so many spoke about in El Salvador and San Salvador. My parents made the decision to leave our birth country during a time of guerrilla war and turmoil, when I was only six months old.

Once in the U.S., my parents understood the power of legal status, so they immediately applied for green cards to receive "legal residency" in the 1980's. By the mercy of God, we qualified and obtained our permanent residency when I was a little child. This allowed my father to work and take care of us financially while pursuing his dream of owning a business—something he was never able to achieve.

While living in East Los Angeles, California, my mother gave birth to four more children, giving me one brother and three younger sisters. All five of us are adults now. Our childhood was fairly "normal" until my parents began fighting, and then abusing us, which led to legal struggles and separation, ultimately resulting in a drastic, life-changing move from California to Colorado in 1992. My parents hoped the move would give their relationship a fresh start. It was then that my life became convoluted, confusing, and dark.

We were different from our new, surrounding community, and I could barely identify with the majority of white kids in my new school. However, my parents found a pocket of Hispanics and immediately rented a home in their neighborhood. During this time of life change, I also continued to live a secret homelife of chaotic abuse. As a small child, I had lived in a constant state of abuse, and now as an older child, I entered a perpetual vicious cycle of observing, hearing, and living trauma firsthand.

However, for some reason, this time it was different; I became lost, mentally. I was unable to run to the safe places in my mind that I had created in California when I was abused. I no longer had my friends, my dreams of becoming famous, my puppies, and my neighbors; things that were more important to a young girl than you would think. I felt ripped away from my life and my safe haven. I became depressed, lost, and suicidal.

I strongly believe that my parents were too young when they got married and moved away from their own safe haven. They were also very immature in the way they saw life. They had the deepest victim syndrome any human beings could have. They clashed personalities and were never satisfied with anything in life. They believed three key things: nothing was ever good enough, bad things always happened only to them--and they would keep happening--and other people or circumstances were always to blame. Any efforts to create change would fail, so there was no point in trying. I had adapted this mindset, and I didn't know it! Eventually, they divorced, and my mother found us a place to live. She survived as a single mother of five kids and my father never reentered the picture.

SAVED FROM MYSELF

During this time, I was unable to understand the many things that happened to me and why, or the bad decisions I made and why I made them. I hated myself and saw myself as the most disgusting, dark soul, undeserving of living or having anything good in this life. My victim mindset was ingrained in my "hard drive." Hate had taken over me as a poor, abused child, and no one knew that the way I sought help was with anger.

Then one day, I was astounded to meet some strangers who

decided to care about me anyway. We lived in the most dangerous projects in the city of Denver, but a gray van would always come by to pick up kids and take them to a nearby kid's church. I discovered faith when I was almost 11 years old. I can't recall how many times I tried to end my life, but God truly saved me. I can't express how thankful I was when I discovered that there was a God willing to have mercy on me and cleanse my soul. I found a healing path to loving myself and I was truly saved! God literally saved my life, and through a long process, he healed me!

Fast forward to my late teens when I began to recognize patterns and constant behaviors that were getting me and my "mouth" into trouble. I applied a law of silence of my own invention. I decided to listen to people and try to care, smile, and be sunshine happy all the time. I decided to learn and analyze human behavior. But there was a time when I was 19 years old, in trouble, and telling lies to protect myself.

What I didn't know was that the person who knew I was lying was hiding behind a door listening to everything I was saying. Suddenly, she popped out and called me a liar in front of the person to whom I was playing victim. It was the best thing to ever happen in my life because it made me realize I was still operating from a victim mindset, too scared to take the blame or face the consequences of my actions. That is when I decided to no longer be a victim. I found help, and a new healing process began in my life.

I entered my first marriage at a very young age and had my first daughter at a very young age. I knew I had to mature and be the best mom in the world. I didn't want my child to have to endure what I did. That is when I learned about the "true love" of motherhood, which became my most amazing reason to fight, work hard, and live. However, as I began to educate myself and prepare for my life as a parent, I was quickly faced with "Jackie" the impostor.

I couldn't find my identity; I was unable to seriously know who I was and why I existed other than to be a mommy to my baby. My first marriage was not what I expected, and I was losing myself. I was so scared! Something in the back of my head always told me that I was created for a purpose, and to impact the world. I had so many dreams, and my heart pumped with so much desire for success. But I didn't want anyone to feel bad as a result of it.

Then one day, I had a vision. I saw myself carrying a huge key and walking up beautiful stairs in the sky. As I reached the end of the stairs, there was an enormous door. I used the key and unlocked the door. As the door opened, I looked through it and saw thousands of leaders saying, "Come on in, it is your time!" Then something in my heart told me to go back to school!

I couldn't believe the vision and the unstoppable urge and motivation I was feeling! But at this point, I lived the incessant mindset of the impostor syndrome where I was in a constant pattern of doubting any accomplishments and even my ability to accomplish anything. I had a persistent, internalized fear of being exposed as a fraud every day of my life. Nonetheless, I obeyed.

I applied and was accepted to my local community college. I did so well that I made the dean's list. I transferred to the

University of Denver and graduated as one of the top students with a bachelor's degree in business administration. I applied to business school at the Daniels College of Business and was accepted. A few years later, I graduated with my MBA. I'm the first one to obtain a graduate degree in my entire family. I humbly say that it was the hardest journey I ever embarked upon because I was simultaneously working full time, raising a child, and going through a divorce.

I knew I had to realize my vision. I continued my journey, and it was difficult as a young, single mother. Somehow, God gave me grace and favor, and I was able to enter through every door that opened and have authority and intelligence to apply what I had learned. My identity, slowly but surely, began to blossom. Although I felt like a fraud throughout my entire university career, I stayed quiet, and still managed to graduate and move on. I was not a fraud, but for some reason I always felt like someone else was better and I was just lucky that I hadn't been caught. The impostor syndrome. It is such a lie!

LEADING FOR LIFE

Life began to teach me that my mission was more powerful than myself. I learned that it was not about me. My understanding expanded as I opened my heart and ended my healing journey by learning to love myself as well as others. I served my community and faith leaders. I started discovering so much within me and I applied it and shared it with everyone who came into my life. I realized that healing came to my life in the form of love and care.

I learned that every shocking life event is a purposeful way for God to open my eyes to see areas for my own self-improvement.

As I reached a more mature and wonderful time in my life, God sent the love of my life, literally, to my door. We had spoken for six months over the phone until one day he drove out to see me so we could have our first date. I remarried and learned what a beautiful, wonderful human being I am. I was able to successfully integrate what I had learned in my new marriage into my career as a professional businesswoman, entrepreneur, and non-profit expert. I sit on two beautiful boards and have successfully spearheaded a strategy that brings hundreds together in Colorado for a greater cause. I'm a Colorado Faith Leader and national representative to the evangelical Colorado Multi-ethnic Coalition and Hispanic faith leaders. I speak in both the business world and the faith world to inspire, motivate, and catapult humans to fearlessly reach their destiny.

I can say that my success is all-encompassing. It includes my childhood, my teens, my young adult life, and now my mature life with a wonderful man and two beautiful babies (with one more on the way). My strong character and maturity only came as a result of my journey and an ability to be humble and open to change. I would venture to say that I have now lost my fear of being a fraud because I believe in myself, and, most importantly, I believe that I was called to do what I do for such a time as this.

REFLECTION QUESTIONS

1. Have you ever felt like an impostor or a fraud? If so, how did you deal with it?

2. Have you known someone who has the victim syndrome? How can you help them?

3. How well do you think you understand your identity?

BIOGRAPHY

Jacqueline Bouvier is an executive director who oversees the Santa Fe Drive commercial corridor in Denver and its evolution of business, physical improvements, and economic development in the past few years. She works closely with stakeholders, executives, and entrepreneurs to build relationships, and focus on economic development and streetscape goals.

After more than a decade working with the community, non-profits, and multimillion-dollar brands and startups, Jackie knows what drives conversions, creates sold-out events, and influences and empowers people. She is considered a world-renowned professional connector and a well-rounded professional in all the areas of engagement, including Bouvier & Co., where she and her husband help non-profits thrive in strategic planning, formation, and governance. She knows how to connect with people's hearts and communicate all understanding back to them.

Jackie has landed coverage in local print magazines, TV, and broadcast outlets around Colorado, including the local radio shows. She is the current president of Prospanica, Denver and a key board member of the Colorado Multi-Ethnic Coalition. She is also a trained business coach and inspirational speaker with an MBA in international studies from the University of Denver with an emphasis on foundations, human resources, and non-profits.

Jacqueline Bouvier
jackieamartz@gmail.com
720-838-8299

Scarleth Lever Ortiz

"The years teach much which the days never know."

I am the oldest daughter of Araceli, a fierce, generous, and resilient mom. In Latin, her name means "altar of heaven." I cannot help but wonder if her name predestined me to find strength and purpose through a higher power.

In 1985, when I was 5 years old, a devastating earthquake shook Mexico City at 7:19 a.m. I remember my dad and I laughing and pretending to skate as the tremor moved us from side to side. My mom was mortified and yelled, "Stop, many people could be dying!" I still remember the event because it was very traumatic. We could not get instant updates of the earthquake's unprecedented damage to the city, so we left home like every other day. When we got closer to the city center, we could see the devastation. That day 10,000 people lost their lives, 30,000 people were injured, and 250,000 lost their homes.

My mom dropped me off with my grandparents and she joined thousands of volunteers who were freeing people from debris, distributing meals, and reuniting families in a pre-internet era. In the days to follow, I joined her, a few times, to distribute hot meals. My most vivid memory was when entire streets were silent and cars were stopped by members of *"Los Topos,"* the moles, a group of volunteers who burrowed into the ruins searching for survivors, to indicate that a potential survivor had been found under the rubble. This experience cemented my desire to help people amid tragedy.

The following year, I spent a summer in Minneapolis with my grandma. I attended kindergarten, but since I did not speak English, the kids made fun of me. I missed home so much. When I returned, my parents separated, and I no longer had a home. We lived with friends until my mom was able to find an apartment.

My mom worked extra shifts to make ends meet, and I became my mom's right hand. I learned to be responsible and care for my two beautiful and smart younger sisters. I also had to maintain good grades to keep a merit scholarship at my private school, so for me, failure was not an option. I had to excel in school and take care of my sisters. Eventually, given all my responsibilities, and an unknown history of anxiety and depression in my family, I began to develop severe anxiety and panic attacks. This is how I was introduced to the fascinating field of psychology, and why cognitive therapy has been (on and off) a part of my entire life. I loved my first therapist, going to her office, and talking about my week's assignments and my worries because I felt safe. I even told my mom I wanted to be a psychologist and she replied, "Absolutely not. They do not make enough money." I wonder if her answer would have been different if she had known how bilingual therapists are in high demand today.

Currently, I am a Diversity & Inclusion practitioner, and I bring awareness to many taboo issues such as racism, sexism, and discrimination. I provide tools aimed at developing empathy, self-awareness, and self-compassion. But my quest to embrace diversity and promote inclusion began much earlier.

INCLUSION STARTS WITH YOU

I grew up in a household of light skinned, blue and green-eyed people. Color is a taboo subject in Mexican society, and the elite are mostly white, or at least light-skinned. Since, the color of my skin and eyes differed from my own sisters and parents, I was asked all the time, *¿Por qué tu no estas güerita?* (Why are you not blonde?). In a society where lightness equals beauty, and I did not see many people who looked like me in the media, my self-esteem began to suffer. In sixth grade, this feeling of exclusion intensified when I learned my dad adopted me, and I met my biological father. I became an angry teenager with no sense of belonging. After graduating high school, I moved to Minneapolis to stay with my grandma and study English.

The move, the cultural shock, the language barrier, and my heavy emotional baggage drove me into a severe depression. I would wake up in the middle of the night, shivering. All I wanted was to go back home, but I did not want to return in defeat. I wanted to accomplish my goal to learn English and overcome my emotional wounds. With the assistance of my therapist, I was able to identify the roots of my painful resentments. By winter break, I chose to forgive, and released my pain and anger. Then, my healing journey began.

People know me as a "talker," so it is hard to believe I refused to speak English until "I mastered" the language. I only read, listened to the radio, and watched TV in English, even when I did not understand. I trusted my grandma who told me if I just kept doing it, I would comprehend. I not only learned English, but I have a minor in French, and lived in Paris for a semester!

I am a nervous test taker, so the results of my standardized tests for college admission were very low. I was accepted to the University of Minnesota, but only in the English as a Second Language (ESL) program. I was supposed to be there for one year but transferred out after the first trimester because my test scores did not reflect my actual skill set. As an undergraduate, I continued to learn English, new concepts and theories, and met students from around the world. I was intrigued by the differences and commonalities of cultures, so I decided to major in international relations and thought about traveling the world as a public servant and mediating political conflicts. After graduation, I visited my sisters and my mom in Mexico, who begged me to stay. I could not. I still had the feeling there was more for me to do.

MAKING OF A PUBLIC SERVANT

My first job was a dream come true. I worked at the American Red Cross and was excited to be with an organization that helped people in crisis. Then, Hurricane Katrina hit. The younger version of me did not understand the politics of the situation and I was disappointed because I was unable to provide direct assistance. Eventually, I quit out of frustration. I moved to Las Vegas and took a position in the marketing department for the elite players of The Venetian casino. There, I discovered the power of money and I realized my true passion was in government. I was fascinated by the energy of different cities and wanted to better understand the role of government, which is responsible for their rise and fall.

I had always loved Chicago's bustling Latinx community, the beautiful architecture, and the Midwest feel. I reconnected with a friend from Mexico who knew me at my worst. After dating long-distance for a year, we married in Las Vegas and drove to Chicago to start our new lives. Since then, he has been my number one cheerleader and has supported me all the way.

My career as a public servant began shortly after I arrived in Chicago. I worked for an alderman and attended graduate school full time. I met the remarkable goal of completing my degree in two years. I also truly found my talents: writing reports, interpreting data, developing workflows, and evaluating programs. While in graduate school, I was able to learn theories and apply them in real-life projects at work using my talents. I attended high-level meetings with powerful decision-makers and was fascinated to witness the impact sole individuals had in the lives of thousands. I learned that if I ever wanted to help someone in crisis, I needed to access power.

Upon graduation, I joined the Chicago Housing Authority (CHA), the second largest housing authority in the nation, where I am the founding director of the Office of Diversity & Inclusion. This year, I celebrated a decade helping low-income families access a safe home.

PEACE AT LAST

In my role as a Diversity & Inclusion practitioner, I met my best friend and mentor, and my journey of self-awareness and self-compassion strengthened. I discovered the power of gratitude and acceptance. It is just as important to evaluate yourself to find ways to improve as much as it is to exercise self-compassion. You should always take time to recharge, to listen to your inner voice, to follow your dreams all while creating strong boundaries. Boundaries are essential to successfully connect with others, especially those who might not understand you. The field of diversity and inclusion prepared me for my spiritual awakening, which happened in the summer of 2017 when I found my current therapist and began to explore the root of the anxiety and perfectionism that prevented me from feeling successful.

In September of 2017, another deadly earthquake hit Mexico City, 32 years after the one I had experienced as a child. For the first time in my life though, I experienced inner peace. I was able to fully engage in the present moment, which included being with my family in Chicago when we learned my loved ones in Mexico City were unharmed. In that moment, the people I cherished most were there with me (both in person and in spirit).

As Thich Nhat Hanh, a Zen leader said, "Life is available only for this moment." In the end, if you do not fully live each moment, you will miss the opportunity to enjoy life. There will always be suffering in the world, but it is up to us to take in the good, the positive. If you search, you will find a purpose and be grateful. When 1 learned about the earthquake, I had to be kind to myself and not internalize how little I could do for the people who were suffering. We each have our own journey and must endure and learn from our sufferings. I have found my purpose in life, which is to find inner peace while always having empathy for others.

As an immigrant, I have always missed home. Life can feel like a hurricane at times. But hurricanes have a center, a center that is quiet and peaceful. That center is your home, and I realize that power lies in finding our center and our inner peace. No one can take the power of inner peace away from you. Exercise self-awareness and self-compassion and you can lead with empathy and unleash your inner power.

Every experience of your life teaches you a lesson. As Ralph Waldo Emerson, a renowned nineteenth-century philosopher said, "The years teach much which the days never know." Everything happens for a reason; our experiences might be different, yet we can find our talents and use our time and treasures wisely to help everyone who crosses our path.

The earthquake in 1985 awoke my desire to help survivors. Feeling excluded and different forced me to explore ways to find everything my heart desires. I am successful because I am grateful for everything I have and use my power with dignity and respect. I am proud to have the privilege to work in government and serve in multiple, mission-driven organizations to always pay it forward.

REFLECTION QUESTIONS

1. How are you using your power?

2. Have you had a spiritual awakening?

3. How do you exercise self-awareness and self-compassion?

BIOGRAPHY

Scarleth is the founding director of the Office of Diversity and Inclusion (D&I) at the Chicago Housing Authority (CHA), the second largest housing authority in the nation serving over 70,000 low-income families in Chicago with an operating budget of $1 billion.

She implemented the Community Alliance, a multicultural and multilingual initiative to increase awareness of CHA's programs among hard-to-reach populations. She re-vamped CHA's language access policy by streamlining the free translation and interpretations services provided to individuals with Limited English Proficiency (LEP). Scarleth also spearheaded many employee-driven activities to commemorate heritage months and awareness of emotional, physical, and psychological health issues.

She is a Leadership Greater Chicago (LGC) Fellow since 2018 and a board-elected member of LGC's Leadership Fellows Association. She serves on the board of Thresholds and the American Civil Liberties Union (ACLU) – The Next Generation Society. Scarleth is also an inclusion strategic advisor for the Illinois Green Alliance.

Scarleth holds a B.A. in Global Studies and minor in French from the University of Minnesota and an M.A. in Urban Planning and Policy from the University of Illinois at Chicago. She is a Certified Diversity Professional (CDP) and an Intercultural Development Inventory Qualified Administrator.

Scarleth Lever
scarlethlever@gmail.com
linkedin.com/in/scarlethlever

Elisa Marquez

"You have the freedom to choose the character you want to be in the story of your life."

Every person in this world has a story: a beginning, end, or "to be continued," a before, an after, and a reason why. There were many times when situations and people hurt me, and I felt they were not fair. Later on, the pieces of the puzzle of life came together to create the whole picture. Your purpose is yet to come; be patient, keep moving forward and the universe will work its way to prepare you for greatness later in life.

My childhood was not a fairy tale. It was full of incidents that shaped my life, with twists and turns that taught me lessons. My teenage years were a roller-coaster of emotions. I started a family early in life, I broke the cycle of generations who were victims of their own decisions, and I compromised with myself to be happy. Every step I've taken, and every fall I've ever had, I've had to choose between staying down and feeling sorry for myself or shaking off the pain and continuing my journey with renewed strength. The hardest times are the ones that have brought me the greatest lessons in life and have helped me become the woman I am today. You can surprise yourself by becoming the best version of yourself.

THE DAD VOID

When I was five months old, my dad unexpectedly passed away at the age of 26. My mom struggled as a widow with two little girls. She was hurt by the loss, but she did not give up-- this was her time to thrive! We were her "why" and she fought for us, with the help of my grandma who took care of us while my mom worked. My mother also attended college while she was employed full time and was able to graduate and become a special education teacher. Without realizing it, I was learning not to give up in life, even if the love of your life passes away and leaves you with two children under two years old.

I missed the father who I never met. At family gatherings, I would see all my cousins with their dads, playing, dancing and receiving affection. I missed what I never had a chance to experience. There was a part of my heart that so wanted to love a dad. My sister and I used to pray for our late dad. We both had an emptiness in our hearts that was ready to be filled, so we started to pray to God to send us a dad.

When I was six years old, my mom met a man who became my stepdad. My sister and I were fortunate to be at their wedding as flower girls, and I remember seeing them at the altar, saying their vows. I felt part of it all, as if it were magic!

I was finally able to experience what it was like to have a dad. He was respectful and caring and wanted to provide for his new family. Later on, we were blessed with two more sisters which my sister and I were happy to welcome into our family. My new dad now had two biological daughters, but he loved all four of us the same, and I respected him for that. I loved him as if he were my own father, and he filled a curious and empty part of my heart.

My new dad used to work in California, and sometimes he would bring us with him for the season. It was a different world, with different people and cultures that were strange to me. However, it helped me begin to learn English and see that there was more out there in the world than what I thought. As a family, we went through financial hardship, but we stayed together and were able to overcome it. As I look back, I can proudly say I never saw or heard my parents fight, nor my dad mistreat my mom, or vice versa. I grew up with parents who talked through their differences and worked together to understand each other. And this example helped me make one of the most important decisions of my life later on.

GROWING UP QUICKLY

During my high school years, I learned to pick my friends carefully. Friendship does not come from hanging out with people at school. Differences, envy, and lots of hormonal changes make it difficult. The ones I called my friends were the ones that mistreated me the most. They would criticize me, or all of a sudden stop talking to each other for no reason other than to make themselves feel important and needed. It got to the point where I preferred to just be by myself; I could not stand the selfishness and arrogance. I decided my friends were not to be found at school, but elsewhere. To this day, I have friends who

I still see who I have decided to keep for life because they are worth it!

When I was 17, I truly fell in love with a man who came into my life before I was ready for him. I was finishing high school and about to start college to study medicine. I had an uncle, very dear to my heart, who was a pediatrician and my doctor growing up. He had inspired me to follow his path. However, my new love convinced me to marry him after graduation, which I did. I was 18 and he was 26 when we wed and moved from my hometown in Mexico, to Chicago, Illinois. I left my life, my family, and my dreams to follow love. He promised that he would help me enroll at one of the best universities in Chicago. I was happy to be with him and he treated me like a queen. I couldn't ask for more!

After a month of marriage, I was pregnant! I was in shock because I was trying not to start a family so soon, but even though it was a surprise, I welcomed the news with open arms and heart. This baby I was carrying was the best thing that could have happened to me. I called it my "little bean," as it looked like that on the ultrasound. I decided I was going to be the best mom I could, even though I was young. I was going to do everything I could to protect and love this baby.

My pregnancy was wonderful, although my marriage was struggling. I thought it was normal since we were newlyweds and we had a baby on the way, and I was determined to work through it. On June 9, a couple of weeks before I turned 19, my daughter Anais was born. The feeling of seeing and holding this little part of you that you carried for nine months and finally get to meet is indescribable; it is the purest love one can feel.

As my baby daughter grew, I asked my husband to support me so I could return to school and study medicine. He said to wait until our daughter was older so she could be raised by me and not others. A year passed and I became pregnant again. This time, unfortunately, after seven weeks of gestation, I had a natural miscarriage. I remember feeling a tremendous pain, not only physically but emotionally; my heart was breaking like it never had before. I had lost my unborn child, and I had to take a couple of weeks to recuperate physically, but more so emotionally. I was depressed and heartbroken for my loss, but I had to go back to being myself again for my daughter Anais who so needed her mom. And so, I lived through my pain and left it behind.

Six months later, I was pregnant again! I could not believe it and was really happy but also apprehensive. I wanted to carry this pregnancy to term. My husband and I were very cautious throughout the pregnancy. We wanted this baby to be part of our family and it happened! Sophia was born when her big sister Anais was two years and ten months old. Anais had no clue what was going on, but she welcomed her baby sister to the family. A year later, as the economy started to crash, I started working to do my part to help the family.

I started as an assistant, working at a bank in the lending department doing mortgages. The following year I was named manager. I was doing great, growing professionally, and enjoying my role. However, the issues which existed between my husband and me before our daughters were born were still ongoing and escalated once I started working. I was really happy being a mom, but unhappy as a wife. I was no longer a teenager, but a woman and mother of two beautiful daughters. My husband and I were not getting along and tried to work it out countless times. I had stopped being myself to please another person, and I was not happy. I was no longer in love, my home didn't feel like a home, and I did not want to raise my daughters in that environment.

THE DECISION

I fell into a deep depression and started having anxiety attacks. Work helped me to forget about my unhappy home, although I needed to take action for me and for my daughters. This was not the life my parents showed me; this was not the example I wanted to show my daughters. I was going to therapy and taking meds for my anxiety and depression. Then one day, on my way to therapy, I had a wakeup call. I looked around as a spectator of my own life and realized I didn't like the part I was playing in it. I wanted to change the script.

I am proud to say that I broke the pattern, the rules, and I decided to be happy and compromise with myself and for my daughters to have a better example of a happy childhood. I do not regret a single decision I made, nor would I do anything different. My decision to get a divorce helped me grow as a woman, a mother, and a professional, and was one of those defining moments that changed the story of my life and left me with no regrets.

My daughters are my "why," and for them, I will do anything. I decided to give them my best, to be happy and make them happy. While working at the mortgage department, I was able to offer them stability by purchasing a house just one year after the divorce. Two years ago, I finished my degree in business management, took online classes while working and being a mom, and graduated with honors. My parents came from Mexico to celebrate this big accomplishment with me, and I made my family and friends proud. I also showed my daughters not to stop dreaming and fighting for what you believe and to be happy and thrive, like my mom once taught me. Now I am my own boss as a mortgage loan consultant, helping families achieve homeownership and helping single moms to get ready to have a home to call their own for their kids.

Life can be defined like a story in a book or a movie; you have the freedom to choose the character you want to be in the story of your life, I decided not to be the spectator, the villain, or the victim. I decided to be my own hero, the warrior that does not give up, the person that thrives through adversity. I have inspired myself to become the women I am today and there is more to come. I will continue being my own cheerleader on my journey to making my own happiness!

REFLECTION QUESTIONS

1. What character are you currently playing in your life story?

2. What compromise do you need to make with yourself?

3. What have you done to inspire yourself lately?

BIOGRAPHY

Elisa Marquez was born in Aguascalientes and raised in Teocaltiche, Jalisco, Mexico. She moved to Illinois when she was 18 years old, where she learned English and began a career in the banking industry. Elisa is a professional expert and consultant in residential mortgage lending at Loan Depot. She has been a licensed loan originator since 2008 and graduated with honors with her B.S. in business management. She is also a strategic leader in managing cross-company team efforts through motivation and mentoring strategies.

Elisa has partnered up with many organizations to financially educate the community. She has held seminars with topics such as "First time homebuyers," "Renovation loans for primary and investment properties," "Know how your credit score works," and "Down payment assistance."

She has also built partnerships with other professionals including attorneys, real estate agents, financial advisors, insurance agents, home inspectors and contractors to help the community handle their finances well and achieve the American dream, homeownership.

Elisa has two daughters, Anais and Sophia, who are the reasons for everything she does. Elisa wants her daughters to enjoy every stage of life as part of the next generation of inspired Latinas.

Elisa Marquez
emarquez@loandepot.com
(312) 401-7001

Gabriela Gomez

"The real definition of beauty is having the strength to continue smiling, even when you don't feel like smiling."

Women come to me, asking me to make them beautiful. They sit in my chair and for the next half hour (or more) I use all of my skill as a hairdresser and cosmetologist to give them the best possible presentation of their exterior. Fabulous hair, long lashes, luscious lips, silky skin. On the outside, they look impeccable.

And while I work, I hear their stories. So many sad stories about how they have been mistreated and victimized by ones who claimed to love them. I feel their sadness, fear, and misery. I can tell they feel unloved, afraid of being alone, dissatisfied with life, tired of unfavorable situations yet unable to emerge from their comfort zone. They are lost.

Coming to me is part of being whole again. They are looking for a change of image or a complete transformation, for a one-time occasion or a reinvention of their look, to change their lives, even for a moment. What they don't know is hearing about their experiences and talking with them has helped me to transform just as much as I have helped transform them!

One day I woke up wanting to write my story to inspire and share what I didn't know that I knew. In this book, I'm given that opportunity and I am forever grateful. And I'll begin at the beginning, where it all started.

LIFE'S EDUCATION

I was born a curious child with a love of learning. Of my ten siblings, I was the only one who pursued education after high school. I always loved to learn new things and still do. Because of that, I've finished different courses of study throughout my life. However, I was never the traditional college student.

College got in line behind life and family. At seventeen I got pregnant with my first baby, and at eighteen, I got married. I soon learned that my idea of love was confused with manipulation and control. I learned that abuse was not only emotional, but verbal too, and that words can destroy the beauty of the illusion of love towards another human being. Pain of physical abuse is not where the bruises show or where the blood runs, but in the soul. I learned that sexual abuse is not an act of love but intimidation that gains strength and breeds fear, that grows like a monster. Then love fades and salty tears shower away the beauty and power of self-love. I learned that the heart, once shattered into pieces, tries to survive each day trying to put each piece back together, and that loving others is the measure of our true self-value.

I'm proud and happy to be the mother of four beautiful children, two beautiful girls and two handsome boys. But after seventeen years of marriage, I finally escaped my abuse with a divorce at the age of thirty-seven. It was then I went to college, majoring in accounting with a minor in business administration. Yet I also always had a deep interest in the beauty industry.

I became a certified, international makeup artist, a licensed cosmetologist, and, finally, a practitioner in neuro-linguistic programming (NLP). NLP is a pseudoscientific approach to communication, personal development, and psychotherapy that professes a connection between neurological processes, language, and behavioral patterns learned through experience. I continued to update myself in the beauty industry and the seemingly unrelated area of neurolinguistics, until one day I had an "aha" moment.

I realized that everything that I have ever studied has filled me with joy, ever since I was a little girl. I remember one of my professors praising me for my intellectual curiosity and academic achievement and encouraging me to continue learning and find different interests. One day, after pulling all of my certifications, diplomas, and licenses together, I thought about what I could do with all of the knowledge I had acquired through the years. What did cosmetology have to do with NLP? Then it came to me. It all added up to BEAUTY.

Cosmetology dealt with external beauty while NLP helped us become our best on the inside, working on our own personal self-development. Internal and external beauty. NLP and cosmetology. I suddenly came up with a great idea and started working on a project to reach as many people as possible, sharing wonderful information regarding their self-image. I was on a mission to help people become their best self, inside and out.

The women in my chair are often just looking for someone to hear them, to vent, and relieve a situation filled with pain, to someone who will not be judgmental. We all fear what family and friends might find out about our reality. Nobody wants to be rejected, neglected, or unaccepted after others find out something about their personal life. They would prefer to continue pretending they are someone they aren't rather than confront their reality.

I don't stop them from venting. I listen to their life stories very closely, very carefully. I observe their gestures, their body language, their emotions and how they run deeply and bloom in different directions. I see how they just want to forget and forgive at times and how ready they are to let go of their past and move ahead of their present to live a better future. But they somehow feel and believe it's impossible.

I can see right through their image and how the true beauty of their essence is absent as they suffer, but yet they want to put a mask on top of their physical body, wanting to hide everything they don't want the world to see. Here is where many seek change, through makeovers and the manipulation of their outer physical bodies. It puts a temporary smile of happiness on their face. They try to find their confidence and courage to feel more powerful by viewing themselves as pretty, stylish, and transformed.

REAL BEAUTY

I used to feel like this too. But now, pursuing my heart's desire, I have learned that the real definition of beauty is having the strength to continue smiling, even when you don't feel like smiling. It's having the faith to accomplish your goals even if they seem impossible and you feel all you have left of yourself is as tiny as a mustard seed, or as minimal as a penny left in your pocket, or as empty as a tiny dot of sand.

Beauty is when your words are as empty as darkness, but you are alive and there is hope to live a better life, to choose what's right for you. Beauty is finding peace within you, to enjoy and meet happiness, and at the end of the day, to encounter success.

Beauty is making the hardest choices at the emotional level and at the end, realizing that what you have accomplished was based on your hardest decision.

Beauty is surviving the unfavorable situations and meeting yourself once again. It's rescuing your soul and giving yourself another chance. It's accepting the strength of your life's choices and decisions.

Beauty is also letting go and enjoying the satisfaction in your child's cute smile, and the loved ones who have walked with you on your journey.

This is why after connecting with so many stories similar to mine, I decided to become educated in personal development to help me understand and rise above my own personal adversity. Once I realized the value of these courses, I put them into practice. Their principles healed me and had an incredible effect on my life. Now I want to share and inspire others through my unique makeup program, which focuses on outer beauty, with skin care and makeup, but also inner beauty, including emotional intelligence and self-image. It is called, "The Art Between the Inner and Outer Beauty."

BETWEEN INNER AND OUTER BEAUTY

I developed this beautiful project based on my personal experience overcoming the effects of my domestic abuse. The principles helped me personally and I knew they would help others as well. I overcame by learning about emotional intelligence, personal growth, staying healthy, and working on my internal beauty, as well as my external beauty. Maintaining both beauties gave me that wonderful enlightenment of my soul and empowered me to develop a program that I now offer to my students who take my personal and professional makeup courses, as well as students in organizations and schools.

My experience as a makeup artist showed me the necessity of connecting both beauties to help my clients maintain confidence, self-esteem, assurance, security, and see themselves as the beauties they are. Instead of focusing on the external mask or the internal cloud and fog within, I help them learn the connection of the wonderful art of inner and outer beauty. I help them release their negativity and change into a suit of positivity that helps them smile from the inside out. In this way, they can explore and discover their new Image!

Believing in myself helped me understand and accept my past story and see everything from a different perspective. My profession as a makeup artist and cosmetologist has opened many doors for me. I was hired to travel to Europe by Jacqueline Camacho, the creator and founder of this book series. She had me do makeup and hair for the authors in Today's Inspired Latinas Volume VI, which led to an invitation to be part of this edition. That amazing opportunity gave me the chance to visit Europe for the first time, and tour Paris, France, Antwerp, and step into Brussels in Belgium. On my way back home, I even stopped in Dublin, Ireland. It was a great adventure and I would like to give special thanks to Jacqueline Camacho for all the great opportunities and for trusting me!

REFLECTION QUESTIONS

1. Can you name three personal priorities?

2. Can you name three personal goals?

3. What can you do today to begin working towards a priority or goal?

BIOGRAPHY

Gabriela Gomez is a licensed cosmetologist, certified international makeup artist and founder of the innovative program, The Art Between Inner and Outer Beauty. She is licensed in several programs, including neurolinguistic programming.

Through her unique beauty program, Gabriela helps her clients combine the elements of outer beauty experienced through her makeup artistry, with aspects of inner beauty, with help from her neurolinguistic training.

Gaby also holds a degree in accounting and is the mother of four young adult children.

Gabriela Gomez
2golddenn@gmail.com
872-237-7275

Angélica Cifuentes Báez

"Body and soul will heal, as long as you heal your mind."

For more than 15 years I have worked as a public accountant and devoted several years of my life to various jobs and a marriage. However, I have always felt a bit disappointed and uneasy coping with some aspects of my life. I've found myself facing tough challenges, feeling like a spectator in life and taking unexpected paths without my intervention. I learned a lot, but it was not easy.

Life is mysterious in pushing its way through, and I had a chance to reveal new truths and adventures when I moved to Montreal, Canada, nine years ago. With the opportunity to apply for a resident visa there, I felt it was an opportunity I should take, even though I didn't know much about the country or the culture, and it was far from home. I arrived full of dreams with a suitcase in hand, eager for a brand-new start with my children. That move was not only physical, but spiritual. That flight not only transported me from one continent to another, but everything inside me started to reorganize and intertwine differently. In some way I was reborn, ready to spring back into shape. I had to learn to speak another language and start to progressively integrate into another culture.

I had divorced and left behind the oppressive relationship that had anchored me for years. My children and I had all undergone a tremendous spiritual and cultural metamorphosis from my divorce, and, after some time, we could collect the first harvest of what we had sowed. Maybe that was one of the first lessons we learned: when you sow healthy seeds and take good care of the abandoned soil, all you have to do is to wait for the beautiful harvest.

At first, I only desired to continue doing what I was used to doing and knew well, so I looked for work as an accountant to support my family. I let the past go, untied my inner laces, removed the dust of my wings, stretched them out, and attempted to fly. In this process I became enlightened about how to share my experience and knowledge with other people.

IN A NEW COUNTRY

Meanwhile, we all worked on starting our new life in another country. My daughter and my son had become the true masters of my universe. I have learned to hear them and be open to receive all their unconditional love.

My challenges were many. I have suffered a lot for not having my mother—Cecilia Báez—closer. She has always been unconditional love to me, a breath of life, and now we were thousands of kilometers apart. As she aged, her memory started failing, however, she was still there, present and unconditional to me, as if her memory could continue as I remembered her. She is an *inspiration-elle* woman. Her wisdom, gentleness, and wholehearted loving has accompanied me all my life. Although she is not the same woman she used to be and is somehow distant, with eyes lacking that knowing look, her smile keeps revealing her mischievous and caring wisdom. Now, every time one of us thinks about the other, in the midst of a huge silence, it is as if we are together and we know our love is intact. She was undoubtedly my first teacher. She is hospitality, refuge, protection, and home.

Another huge challenge was living in a world that did not speak my mother language. It was hard to internalize that the only unavoidable path for me was to learn theirs. It is a seed, a starting point, to attempt a new life as a foreigner. You can get work by simply babbling, but in the end—hopefully earlier rather than later—you must return to the seed, because you need to grow. I discovered both English and French, and my world quickly expanded.

GROWTH THROUGH LANGUAGE

After learning French, I met lots of people from other communities different from mine, and my social life changed completely. I learned about community service and started to appreciate certain aspects of life I did not know about. I discovered that fear is always present, and we must get used to it, even if we do not understand why. Survival, challenges, disappointments, everyday struggles, unhealthy relationships, and hypocrisy are other baggage that nobody sees. Surprisingly, I got to know myself differently and I realized I was capable of great growth and I should loosen the chains that prevent me from flying. I still fly, keep learning, and now I can land and take off again successfully. This weird balance untangled my own structure, because now I can better enjoy the walk, the challenges, and the achievements. Now I know how to live without fear.

After learning French, I started to learn English. It was not only essential to pursue further development, but also to get involved with other people and circumstances. I stopped worrying about my accent when I realized I had to honor my roots by not denying my origin or who I was. I also am my accent. I really appreciate the chance to share my heritage with people from other parts of the world who speak a different language, so I can grow closer to them and learn even more about myself. They all nourish me.

Nobody told me what to do. I reinvented, questioned, and transformed myself. I keep flowing and living a plentiful life, overcoming adversities with love and patience, and always making the best of every situation. Now I can say I am happy to be here sharing this transformational process with my kids. I have been blessed with love and I have a Canadian partner that could not be more kind-hearted. Together, we are deliberately shaping our way through life along with our children.

PEACE THROUGH BODY AND SOUL

Today, I can tell you that body and soul will heal, as long as you heal your mind. Peace does not come by itself; you have to pray for it with intention and patience. You have to weather the storm, or wait for it to pass, because after moments of pain, there comes a sunrise. You will certainly wake up more calm, energetic, humble, and thankful. Gratitude has been the magic vitamin that fueled the whole process, even when I no longer want to live. I thought my life was a nightmare, and I was unable to say thank you... but why? I used to think I had nothing to be thankful for since my life was complete chaos, darkness, sadness, and despair. It was not until I delved deeper into my heart to discover the cause of my unhappiness. It was all about the burden of my life story.

One day I woke up with the intention to look into what was hurting me and making my life such a struggle. I needed that dose of gratitude that would give me the strength to do it. Once in my new place with my old scars, I cleaned my knees and stood up stronger. Little by little, while walking this new path, I started putting together the pieces of my own story into the big puzzle with the strong conviction that there was something else feeding my will. I dare say I had some doubts about just letting the divine force guide my way. I did not want to lose control of my life. But signals became unmistakable and the wake-up call grew louder.

Women were definitely entering my life who were the missing pieces that would give me the support to appreciate my puzzle. Those women were there to provide the material I needed to refurbish my own life. Without hesitation, I said YES to that call and to a purpose that defines my life as it is today and makes me plunge in without being scared, to set ablaze in the torch of never-ending wisdom.

BETTER TOGETHER

"Together we get farther" has been the motto that drove me to gather women who were willing to tell their stories and inspire others. I have always believed women should complement, not compete with each other. I called them to be part of a group called Inspirationelle, borrowing the word "elle" from French, which means woman. There, women are free from any prejudices, and the group is a place they can create, innovate, and feel the freedom of being unique and true to themselves as they evaluate their path in life. It's a magic place where they feel confident to share and learn, and I give them tools to develop skills. We learn together and I am just a simple match, striking a torch to walk down the path--a path that is not always so smooth and sometimes unknown. However, we are certain that the path will lead us to find the real truth.

I have become a guide in this journey to give support to these women and help them step up when they fall. I encourage them to find the light for the torch that connects us to our inner wisdom, and the key to our unity. I found passion in walking alongside others in their journeys, and that has cured me. Now, I cannot help but follow the call to serve so many women that need to awaken themselves as I have done.

I have gained further knowledge and wisdom through personal development and I am guided by the Force of Creation that drives my way and lights my torch. I started to understand self-compassion and how to love myself and others. And I realized that while healing myself, I could help other people heal.

I have come across so many questions from women of different origins, races, ages. Thus, I thought my words might help so many others or just make them ask themselves, should my life change direction? Why should I change myself and not others?

I would like to invite all women to get together, meet with ourselves, and honor our uniqueness. Our passion, happy moments, fears, grief, and loneliness sometimes makes us weak. However, today I invite you to share your experiences and call your inner force to wake up, grow, and prepare for a new flight that will be lighter, consistent, and liberating. Before we can fly, we need to learn how to take off and how to land by getting rid of any prejudices and discrimination. Each of you, carrying your torch, can make your heart blaze. I will be waiting for you, fire of inspiration.

REFLECTION QUESTIONS

1. Have you given yourself permission to dream about the life you deserve?

2. What fear prevents you from being yourself?

3. What would happen if you could show the best of your essence to all you meet?

BIOGRAPHY

Angélica Cifuentes Báez is Colombian and has lived in Montreal, Canada, since 2011. She is truly passionate about raising awareness about the role of women in society. She has rendered services as a public accountant for more than fifteen years.

Gradually, she discovered personal development and became so intrigued that she left her career to devote herself completely to the study of human beings from a holistic approach by training as a neuro-linguistic programming (NLP) coach and naturotherapist. She then decided to cultivate her faith in God and spirituality, and learned more about quantum physics and other related disciplines to complete what Angelica calls the first cycle of her master's degree (the purpose of life) in the university of life.

She has devoted herself to helping others through workshops, meetings, and other activities with like-minded women. She creates communities and loving environments which are free from judgment. She has a special passion for nature, where she can feel the freedom of being genuine to herself. Her message is that you should give yourself permission to know who you are from inside out so that your light can blaze fiercely.

Angélica Cifuentes Báez
acifuentesbaez@gmail.com
+1 (438) 939-6690

Carolina Rojas

"True success is within us."

Ever since I was a kid, I've always had a tendency to help others. It filled me with joy to know I could have an impact on somebody. That's when my longing to be a servant of the people began.

Of course, when I was very young, sometimes when I wanted to help, I just got into a lot of trouble. Maybe it was because I wanted to get involved in things that weren't any of my business, like my parents said. But I did it with a humble heart, and in my opinion, to improve circumstances. That's when I also learned that lending a helping hand also has limits. It's necessary to recognize when people are open to support, but equally important to accept when they are not.

MY ROLE MODELS

I thank my parents infinitely for the principles and values they instilled in me from a young age; they have helped me so much to this day. I am Colombian, and I was born into a loving family in a very rural part of the country. That's why I really like freedom and the fresh outdoors. I am so proud of my heritage and history. I love and respect cultures, religions, and politics. I feel the Latino culture has a wonderful mix of strength, freedom, temperance, and persistence, with wonderful principles and values. We have a rich texture to our culture and language. It's also why I love when someone, a Latina woman for example, is persistent and does not allow herself to be subjugated by economic, cultural, social, or educational constraints. M y mother is a role model for me who has shown excellent passion and strength throughout my lifetime. From a young age, I noticed how hard she worked for our family. Growing up, my father was a military pensioner and we relocated to the capital city for his job. My parents moved there with their three children, without knowing a soul.

We arrived in a very humble neighborhood of the capital. Even though my father provided for us, his income was not enough. My mother was a housewife and did not work outside the home or have higher education. For my low-income family, the idea of attending a university wasn't realistic. However, my mother was always very enterprising, although she had never sold a thing in her life up to that point.

One day, my mother was offered the opportunity to attend a meeting of Yanbal, a great beauty products company. She was impressed with the very excellent quality of the merchandise, but could not buy them. So, they offered her a business opportunity to begin a career in Yanbal and have access to the products. Through selling the products and offering others the opportunity to also partner with Yanbal if interested allowed my mother to make some additional income.

She spoke to my father, and my father didn't believe in her.

He thought she wasn't going to get very far and agreed to let her work, but said, "Everything in the home must be kept the same." So that's what my mother did.

She worked very hard and delegated chores to us to help her at home. All the efforts were worth it, because she earned three times what my dad earned as an employee. She managed to climb as high as she could in the company in the first year, and they gave her our first car. It was such an unforgettable moment for our family.

Shortly thereafter, she invited my father to retire from his job and go work with her. That's how they started their successful entrepreneurial journey together. Between the two of them, they built a very nice business and career and have been operating for more than thirty-one years in Colombia. They were able to travel to over thirty-eight countries and always stayed in five-star accommodations, courtesy of the company.

From a young age, I also developed a deep faith in God, thanks to my mother's influence. She showed me the way to God and I received a strong foundation and virtues for life. To me, this was even more important than what I learned at a school or university. My mother laid the foundations of faith in our home, and a big part of that was putting faith into action. Our faith is not only what we feel or what we believe is right, but what we put into practice. We need to ask ourselves, what can we do to serve others and put our values and faith into action?

I saw this firsthand in how my mother served our family in such an exemplary way. My mother put her faith into action within her work, and upheld her value of servitude.

Between my parent's hard work and their entrepreneurship in Yanbal, they were able to give me the opportunity to attend elementary and secondary schools as well as university. I feel very fortunate to have been able to study, and even more so because of all the hard work my parents did for my siblings and me.

Today, all of my siblings are professionals with great careers. In my previous profession, I worked with one of the largest scientists in my country on a vaccine formulation. I had great examples at home who always worked hard and fought to go further, both personally and professionally.

NEW OPPORTUNITIES

While I was studying chemistry at my university, and starting my career my mother continued her business in Yanbal. I watched as my mother kept growing and simultaneously offering that opportunity to others. I watched as she mentored many women who needed additional income, and taught them how to create their own companies within Yanbal. I watched and realized that the only way someone could grow was by helping others grow. I decided to try this out because I saw how many people needed extra income, and I wanted to help. That's when I decided to join the opportunity in Yanbal. I saw an excellent opportunity to help other people who did not necessarily have the opportunities they needed to succeed and truly make an impact in their lives. I joined this great adventure in this wonderful enterprise, and worked alongside my mother for more than ten years. In the beautiful work that we do, I've learned a lot and developed as a professional.

I'm proud of my own personal development over the years. I learned to awaken and bring out the talents I have inside me. With that realization, I had the joy of helping so many people around me encounter the same joy. I love helping women see their untapped potential and beauty inside. I am also happy to promote such world-class personal care products, that are totally natural but developed with high technology, and have lasting short, medium, and long-term positive effects.

First, we help them look good physically, and then we coach them to feel good inside. After they feel good, they can give their best to their environments. After they can give their best to their environments, they discover their real talents. Discovering their talents allows them to gain confidence, begin to lead others, and succeed in their own entrepreneurial endeavors. Once they achieve success, they in turn help more people who want to become entrepreneurs. Outside of making others feel good about themselves, Yanbal also is very profitable. Many women have been able to travel the world without a cost to them and received other perks such as cars, awards, other incentives, and recognitions.

For me, being part of this work is definitely my mission in life. Some will tell you this is a job, and I say it isn't. It's more than that; it's my life mission and on this life mission, I give lots of credit to my mother. I don't see numbers in my work, but I see an impact on people. I see that apart from the compensation, Yanbal has helped bring about a change in their lives. It's truly a wonderful transformation, just like when the small pupa becomes a beautiful, colorful butterfly.

My passion in life is definitely to serve, as I mentioned in the beginning. I feel fulfilled and happy when I serve. I feel that happiness is not so much in receiving, but in giving. I'm happy when I see a beautiful smile in front of me. I am happy when I see that a person feels secure, and has developed greater self-esteem. When they have received a "You can do it!" or when they have received training to explore their talents. When they use those talents to get ahead. That, for me, is a wonderful opportunity to serve that has been built on a commitment to serve others as a life-long project.

LIFE-LONG LEARNING

My journey hasn't always been easy. I've had some tough times, and I can share that everything hasn't always been perfect. There are times when I have felt weak, and perhaps unable to do some work. But these moments should help us learn not to repeat our mistakes, and to be very careful not to be tempted by things in life that are unhelpful, or even damaging. Principles and values must prevail, but of course we are human and sometimes it is part of life to fall.

One of the most difficult things for me to see is other people's suffering. I've met damaged women who think their problems have no solution. For me, seeing their low self-esteem, damage from their parents, or abuse from others, is never easy. Those first moments of contact, seeing their overwhelming realities, is difficult. When I go home, it's a challenge to visualize and establish an action plan with each of them. I understand how they feel and empathize with them. That's why I fight too, letting them know they have my support and I believe they are capable of greatness.

I've seen thousands of testimonies from women who have overcome their past lives. They've counted on me and we've built life-long friendships. I work hard to teach women that with me they will have a guide to take them step by step into achieving everything they want. There is no greater satisfaction than seeing them achieve goals and realize the evolution they've had in their lives.

The most beautiful thing, however, is seeing the change in their environments, their families, and their children. Their evolutions transcend beyond themselves as they become examples for others. This gives me more assurance that I am polishing my craft and methods, and also becoming a true friend and mentor. Together, we learn daily, and that's priceless for me.

My mother has now retired to pursue her humanitarian and social work and left me in charge of the business completely. We merged my mother's business and mine, and right now we're Colombia's biggest business in our company. We have about 35,000 women who take part in our organization. They are 35,000 families that continue to grow and expand every day across the country. In the U.S., we have 250 families because we just started our work there four years ago.

This experience has become my mission in life, not only in

my contribution to help and create careers for people, but also to see how all the things being generated have created a wonderful impact with our work. It has been absolutely phenomenal to see the growth that we have generated. It shows that growth is possible when we use the talents that each individual has been given.

It fills me with pride to train people and look at their journeys with personal development. For me, my desire is not only to testify to my own success, but also support the thousands of testimonies from people who have accompanied me in my career of almost 25 years. I have seen so many life transformations. It's amazing to watch someone go from having no home to owning five of them. To watch someone who didn't have a car because they couldn't drive, to now having 10 cars.

It's been a wonderful experience—but I repeat—everything starts with personal growth. True success is within us, and we must always remember that serving is like living. When you help others, life will reward you with thousands of blessings when you least expect them.

REFLECTION QUESTIONS

1. Who are you currently serving and what impact are you having on them?

2. What life-long fundamental principle or value are you living out in your everday work?

3. How can you grow personally in order to serve people better?

BIOGRAPHY

Carolina Rojas is a happy woman with a passion for helping others and making people around her happy. She studied Chemistry at the National University of Colombia and had the opportunity to work in various entities in research, development, and quality control processes. She had the opportunity to also work at the National Institute of Immunology along with the prestigious Colombian scientist Manuel Elkin Patarroy.

However, what she really considers her vocation has been helping empower women to believe in themselves again and assisting them to find their own talents that they carry within. Carolina is an Elite Diamond Director of the global multi-level company Yanbal International. Carolina considers herself a talent hunter, as she wears 'glasses' that not many have, to be able to see the interior and potential of each person and empowers and trains them to become successful entrepreneurs and generators of successful companies with the support of Yanbal. She came to the United States five years ago to continue expanding her enterprise and develop leaders in Yanbal USA. Carolina is a dedicated mother, head of the household, and has two wonderful children. She has been an entrepreneur for over 20 years and has enjoyed all the amazing benefits that she has reaped during her career.

Carolina Rojas
carolinaoportunityyanbal@gmail.com
@yanbalusaonline

Jacqueline S. Ruíz

**ENTREPRENEUR, AUTHOR, SPEAKER, PILOT,
TODAY'S INSPIRED LATINA FOUNDER**

BIOGRAPHY

Jacqueline S. Ruíz is a visionary social entrepreneur that has created an enterprise of inspiration. Her keen sense of service coupled with the vision to bring good to the world have led her to create two successful award-winning companies, establish two nonprofit organizations, publish over 20 books, create many products, and has held dozens of events around the world in just the past decade.

She is often referred to as a "dream catcher" as her strategies have supported thousands of women, authors and young ladies to live a life of significance. Jacqueline's quest to be a servant leader extends to every area of her life. She has shared her inspiration in four continents and aligned with some of the most powerful brands to elevate others. At only 37 years of age, she has achieved what most would not do in an entire lifetime. Being a cancer survivor sparked a sense of urgency to serve and transcend.

Jacqueline believes that magix (yes, a made-up word that means magic x 10) is the interception of profit and impact. She is one of the few Latina sports airplane pilots in the United States and will soon embark on the historic air race that 20 women flyers participated in crossing the United States 91 years ago, including the famous Amelia Earhart.

Jacqueline believes that "taking off is optional, landing on your dreams is mandatory."

For more information, visit www.jackiecamacho.com.

Made in the USA
Monee, IL
04 November 2020

46698258R00105